Homelessness

Independence
Educational Publishers
Cambridge

First published by Independence
PO Box 295
Cambridge CB1 3XP

British Library Cataloguing in Publication Data
Homelessness – (Issues for the Nineties Series)
I. Donnellan, Craig II. Series
362.5

ISBN 1 86168 020 1

Printed in Great Britain
at City Print Ltd
Milton Keynes

Typeset by
Claire Boyd

Cover
The illustration on the front cover is by
Andrew Smith / Folio Collective.

CONTENTS

Chapter One: No fixed abode

Chapter Two: Runaways

Introduction

Homelessness is the fifth volume in the series: **Issues For The Nineties**. The aim of this series is to offer up-to-date information about important issues in our world.

Homelessness looks at the plight of the homeless in various sections of the community, including the young, the elderly and families. The book also explores the issue of runaways.

The information comes from a wide variety of sources and includes:
Government reports and statistics
Newspaper reports and features
Magazine articles and surveys
Literature from lobby groups
and charitable organisations.

It is hoped that, as you read about the many aspects of the issues explored in this book, you will critically evaluate the information presented. It is important that you decide whether you are being presented with facts or opinions. Does the writer give a biased or an unbiased report? If an opinion is being expressed, do you agree with the writer?

Homelessness offers a useful starting-point for those who need convenient access to information about the many issues involved. However, it is only a starting-point. At the back of the book is a list of organisations which you may want to contact for further information.

*****

Young people and homelessness

Definition of youth homelessness

Besides young people sleeping rough, youth homelessness includes those living in temporary accommodation such as hostels, squats or bed-and-breakfast hotels. It also includes young people staying temporarily with friends and relatives who are unwilling or unable to accommodate them in the longer term.

How many young people are homeless?

The Department of the Environment (DoE) publishes quarterly bulletins on the number of officially homeless households – those to whom councils have a housing duty. These include households with members who are vulnerable through old age, mental illness, physical disability or other special reasons; households with dependent children or with a pregnant woman; or households made homeless through emergencies such as flood or fire. Most young homeless people do not fall within these groups and therefore

Information from Shelter

are not eligible for housing under the homelessness legislation, which means they are not counted in the Government homelessness figures.

Evidence shows that youth homelessness is a national problem. A report by the National Inquiry into Preventing Youth Homelessness, 1996, estimates that in 1995 at least 246,000 young people became homeless in the UK. The Inquiry states that the number of young homeless people is increasing.

Around a quarter of single homeless people sleeping rough or living in hostels or bed-and-breakfast hotels are under 25 years of age (Anderson I, Kemp P, and Quilgars D, *Single Homeless People*, Department of the Environment, HMSO, 1993).

Almost 6,000 single homeless people were referred to Stonham Housing Association during the first six months of 1995 and over half (55%) of these were under 25 years of age (*The Inquiry into Preventing Youth Homelessness*, CHAR, 1996).

Over half the single people applying as homeless in Hull in 1993/4 were under 25 years of age and accounted for just over 2% of the young population of Hull (*Lives of the young and homeless in Humberside*, Save the Children, 1994).

Who becomes homeless?

Young homeless people come from a wide variety of backgrounds. A survey conducted by the St Mungo Association in London found that almost half of its residents in hostels, care homes and halfway houses had academic qualifications, a quarter had 'O' levels or GCSEs, one in ten was educated to A-level standard and a further tenth had a degree (St Mungo's press release and statistical analysis, May 1996).

Certain groups such as women, young gay men and lesbians, care leavers and young people from black and other ethnic minorities are more vulnerable to homelessness. Within London, Centrepoint is one agency that provides specialist help for young homeless people. A recent survey found that nearly half (48%) of the young people admitted into its hostels were from black and ethnic minority groups (*The New Picture of Youth Homelessness in Britain*, Centrepoint, 1996).

Why are so many young people homeless?

Unemployment and pay

Young people can be trapped in a cycle of homelessness and unemployment. Without work it is difficult to find a place to live but it is almost impossible to get a job without a permanent address. In spring 1996, the unemployment rate for 16 to 24-year olds was around 15% – roughly twice the national average (*Labour Force Survey Quarterly Bulletin*, HMSO, 1996). Many of those in work were in part-time or insecure jobs with low incomes. This lack of certainty can make it difficult to get a home.

Even young people in full-time employment may not be able to afford housing. Most young people are on low wages, earning on average between £126.70 and £242.60 per week (dependent upon age and gender) compared to the average for all ages which is £348.50 (*New Earnings Survey*, 1996). In April 1995, the average rent for a one-bedroom home in London was £153.59 which is therefore beyond the reach of many young working people (*Private Sector Rents Bulletin*, London Research Centre, No 10). The cost of good housing means that young people are forced into cheaper options such as renting a room in a house that has been divided into small flats, studio flats and bedsits. These are known as Houses in Multiple Occupation (HMOs). They can carry increased fire risks and are generally of poor quality.

Benefits

Since 1988 most unemployed 16 and 17 year-olds have not been automatically entitled to income support unless they are undertaking Youth Training. However, there are not enough Youth Training places for all of them. If living independently, 16 and 17 year-olds may claim a discretionary hardship payment but these are difficult to obtain and are only awarded for a few weeks at a time.

The number of 16 and 17 year-olds who successfully made new claims for severe hardship payments in a given month has risen from 1,669 in May 1990 to 10,376 in April 1996 (Youthaid, 1996). Despite this increase, 42% of the young people arriving at Centrepoint hostels in 1995 had no income whatsoever (*Annual Statistics*, Centrepoint, 1995).

From October 1996, the Job Seekers Allowance (JSA) replaced income support and unemployment benefit for those who have to register for work. Income support was previously paid to young people between 18 and 25-years of age at a reduced rate although those claiming unemployment benefit received the full rate. The JSA is paid at a reduced rate for all 18 to 25 year-olds who are eligible. This means that some young people who were claiming unemployment benefit will suffer a cut in benefits. However, they face the same costs of living, rent, food, travel, fuel bills and so on as older people.

Housing benefit is only paid in full up to a local reference rent set by Rent Officers. The local reference rent for private rented homes is based on the size and location of the dwelling. Where the rent for a property is above the local reference rent, housing benefit will only cover half the difference between the local reference and actual rent. The local reference rent for single people under the age of 25 is based on shared not self-contained accommodation. For some young people shared accommodation is not a suitable option. If a young person on housing benefit takes up self-contained accommodation after October 1996, they will have to pay the remaining from their own income or face eviction.

The poverty trap

When a person receiving benefits starts work, the combined effect of benefit withdrawal, national insurance and income tax means that real income is reduced at almost the same rate as earnings increase. Unless the earnings are substantially above the value of the benefits, people may end up worse off by working, once costs such as travel and clothing are taken into account.

Leaving care and nowhere to go

Care leavers become independent much younger than most other young people, often with little or no support from family and friends. They do not enjoy the option of occasionally returning 'home' to be looked after. Young care leavers are often expected to cope on their own immediately and may not have had the opportunity to learn life skills such as budgeting and housekeeping.

Under the Children Act 1989, social service departments have duties and powers to provide accommodation and support to care leavers. However, a shortage of funding and the discretionary status of many of the provisions, mean the quality of service is inconsistent. For example, around a quarter (23%) of young people leaving care say they had no support from any source (*Prepared for Living: Leaving Care Research Project*, University of Leeds, 1992).

With a lack of support young care leavers are more likely to become homeless. A DoE study in 1991 found that over half the 16 and 17 year-olds and 39 % of 18 to 24 year-olds living in temporary accommodation had lived in care, hospital or other type of institution at some point previously (*Single Homeless People*, HMSO, 1993).

Forced to leave home

Recent research by Centrepoint with 7,500 homeless young people in seven different locations across the country found that 86% had been forced to leave home rather than choosing to leave (*The New Picture of Youth Homelessness*, Centrepoint, 1996). Reasons included:

- family arguments
- relationship breakdown
- overcrowding
- physical and sexual violence.

In 1991, a study by CHAR found that four in ten homeless young women had suffered sexual abuse prior to becoming homeless (*Four in Ten*, CHAR, 1992).

The Government has argued that young homeless people should return to their families rather than rely on social security. This is in spite of the evidence that the majority do not have homes to go back to.

Asylum seekers
In 1995, the Refugee Council housed 2,591 asylum seekers and refugees and 48% of these were between 17 and 25 years of age. During 1996 the Government passed the Asylum and Immigration Act 1996 which curtails the housing and social security rights of asylum seekers who do not apply at the port of entry and those who are appealing against the refusal of their application. This will leave many young people who have already suffered traumatic exper-iences before coming to this country destitute and reliant on charitable donations and community provision.

Discrimination
Within society young people are often stereotyped as feckless and irresponsible. This can affect their ability to find somewhere to live. Minority groups face added discrim-ination. In 1989, the Commission for Racial Equality found that one in five accom-modation agencies were consistently discriminating against black clients. The Commission also found that a local authority had housed white homeless families far quicker than black families with the same housing needs. Many lesbians and gay men suffer harassment and abuse due to their sexuality and have to leave their homes. Almost half of those applying to Stonewall, a London housing association for young lesbians and gay men, said that harassment by landlords, neighbours and others was a factor in their homelessness (*The Inquiry into Preventing Youth Homelessness*, CHAR, 1996). Young disabled people also face severe accommo-dation problems because of the lack of adequate housing. In April 1995, there were only 147,761 disabled access homes in England.

• The above is an extract from *Young People and Homelessness*, published by Shelter. See page 39 for address details.

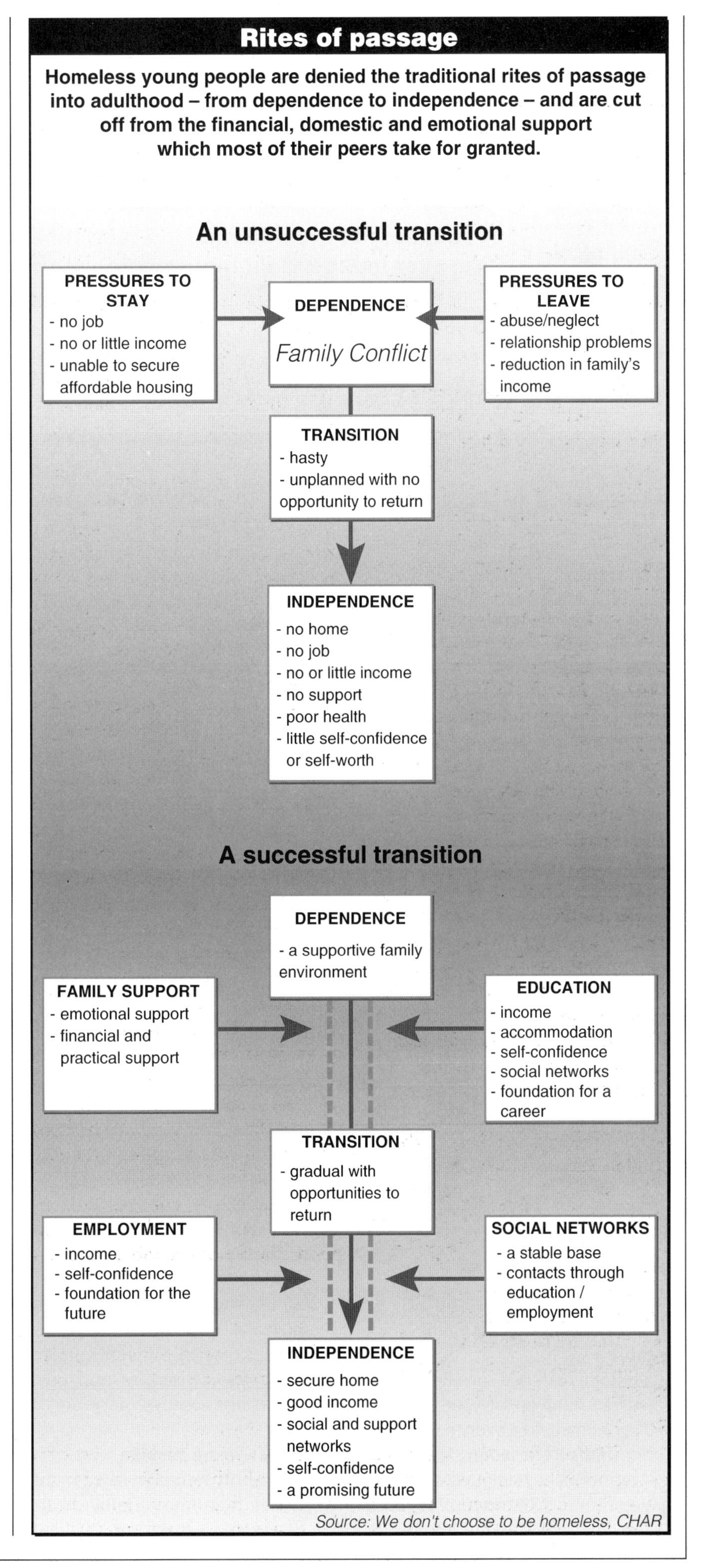

Source: We don't choose to be homeless, CHAR

'We don't choose to be homeless'

A summary of the findings and recommendations of the first ever independent inquiry into youth homelessness

Homeless 16 to 25 year-olds

- do not generally choose to leave home
- are from all walks of life and every region of Britain
- are a vulnerable and neglected group
- represent an immense human and financial cost.

The result?...
broken dreams, unnecessary misery and unfulfilled potential.

In essence...
'Thousands upon thousands of young lives are being wasted, yet so much could be done to help them.'

Andreas Whittam Smith,
Chairman of the Inquiry.

Put another way...
'How many beatings do you have to take before you're justified in leaving home...?'

'All I want is somewhere safe and secure to live, a job, and people who care about me...'

'You can't do anything when you're not eating: you feel so tired...'

'I feel incapable, frustrated, alone and confused...'

Or in figures...
Between 200,000 and 300,000 young people in Great Britain experienced homelessness in 1995.

The facts in more detail

Homelessness among young people...

- is not a marginal social problem. Large numbers of young people are homeless in every part of the country. The young homeless cannot be stereotyped. Neglect, abuse, poverty and ethnic origins can all be factors; but even those from privileged backgrounds can experience homelessness. For some it is a temporary crisis, for others a recurring state.
- is a hidden and neglected problem. It is not considered a 'priority need'. It affects, in particular, a growing band of vulnerable teenagers, aged 17 and under, who slip through the limited statutory safety net.
- can be eased in many areas without spending very much more. At the core of the solution lies public and political recog-nition that there is a major problem, and that we all bear a responsibility in finding answers.
- will be much more difficult to put right in the future if we do nothing now. By ignoring the plight of young homeless people, we undermine the principles and core values of a caring society.

Homeless young people...

- are mainly forced to leave home rather than choosing to do so. Stress and escalating tensions, caused by poverty at home, or by a change in the family structure, can make life intolerable. Some young people are simply shut out. 40% of young women who become homeless have experienced sexual abuse in childhood or adolescence.
- are not only without a proper home, but are hopelessly caught in the poverty trap. With no or very little income, it is more likely that if homelessness continues, young people will turn to petty crime and prostitution, leading to drug and alcohol abuse. Their physical and mental health quickly deteriorates.
- are disproportionately represented by care leavers – a particularly vulnerable group. Research shows around 90% of care leavers to be unemployed, compared with 15% of all young people... around a quarter of young people leaving care (23%) indicated in a recent study that they had no support from any source.
- have few housing options open

to them. Youth unemployment has risen alarmingly, while reduced benefits do not readily support independent living. Even a job does not guarantee independence: youth pay is low and has dropped relative to average wages in recent years.
- will often need practical, as well as emotional support.

What needs to be done . . . because something can be done

Developing effective local strategies

- A national network of local strategic forums should be established to provide a vehicle for action and both a framework and a spur to change. (This conclusion is reinforced in research for the Inquiry by McKinsey and Company – see appendix 5 of the full report.)
- Local authorities, health authorities, voluntary agencies and even local business must work together to develop effective homelessness strategies, tailored to their area's specific needs.
- Local authorities, housing associations and voluntary agencies must work together to review policies on waiting lists and allocation, low-demand accommodation like high-rise flats, shared accommodation and accessibility to the private sector.
- 16 and 17 year-olds must be recognised as a priority group under housing legislation. Local authorities must fulfil their duties under the Children Act and must be penalised when they do not.

Supporting care leavers into independence

- Statutory and voluntary agencies must make sure that those leaving care, or other institutions, are adequately prepared and supported; and able to find the sanctuary of a suitable environment when they are in difficulty.

Reinstating an equitable benefits system

- Income support levels should be returned to the same level as for those over 25. The present discrimination which assumes a certain amount of dependence on family resources should stop.
- Benefit rules should be amended to allow young people to return to full-time education.

Prioritising and measuring the problem

- Youth homelessness must be seen as a national priority with a ministerial working party to examine the problem. It should be audited and monitored by all local authorities and included in housing need projections.

Preventative education

- The implications of leaving home and fending for one's self should be included in secondary school and youth work curricula.
- There should be a comprehensive and accessible advice and information service for young people, ideally with out-reach advice, support and advocacy services.

Family support and mediation

- Family mediation services should be established in all areas to help prevent homelessness and help families renew and maintain contact after disputes.
- Parents should be made more aware of the need to support their children through the difficult transition from dependence to independence.

'There is no single cause . . . and no single magic solution . . . but the Inquiry Members are certain that the range of measures we propose will dramatically reduce the levels of youth homelessness.'

Andreas Whittam Smith,
Chairman of the Inquiry

Ordering the report . . .

The full report *'We Don't Choose to be Homeless'* is available from CHAR, 5–15 Cromer Street, London WC1H 8LS, priced at £17.50 per copy including package and postage. Please state the title and quantity clearly when you order and make your cheque payable to CHAR.

Source: Centrepoint

1 in 20 of young are homeless

The biggest-ever inquiry into homelessness has revealed the shocking truth that *one* in *twenty* British youngsters has no proper place to live.

Caught in the poverty trap and forced to leave home, more than 300,000 desperate young people aged between 16 and 25 had to sleep rough or beg for room at friends' houses last year.

The damning figures also show that a growing number of young women are being forced onto the streets. Sixty per cent of the homeless in Birmingham, for instance, are women.

The inquiry, commissioned by nine charities including Barnardo's, Shelter, the YMCA, YWCA and NCH Action for Children, shows the problem is a national disgrace.

Figures collected by the YMCA, for instance, show that 140,937 young people aged between 16 and 25 in Britain's urban areas are actually on the street.

A massive 315,743 – one in ten – are either on the streets or living in unsuitable accommodation.

The most common reasons for youngsters sleeping rough are conflict at home, poverty, abuse and having to leave care homes at 18.

Another survey, by the charity Centrepoint, of 7,500 homeless youngsters across the country showed that 86 per cent had been forced to leave home rather than leaving of their own accord.

Poverty added to the strain – one in three children is now growing up in poverty-stricken families compared with one in ten in 1979. Andreas Whittam-Smith who headed the inquiry said: 'It is all too easy, once homeless, to slide into a life of petty crime, drug or alcohol abuse, or prostitution.'

The report claims the Government's 'safety nets' – the Children's Act 1989, homelessness legislation and community care legislation – are failing the young.

Priority

'There is evidence that many local authorities don't rank youth homelessness as a priority issue,' says the report, released yesterday at the launch of Youth Homelessness Week.

Across the country, 350 housing-related organisations which were involved in the survey, revealed that homelessness among young people is growing at a faster rate than in any other group.

A quarter of single, homeless people sleeping rough or living in hostels or bed-and-breakfast hotels are under 25. The inquiry has drawn up a six-point plan which it claims will help the needs of young people – and save taxpayers up to £2,400 per person over two years.

More support is needed for youngsters leaving care, it says.

Local authorities which don't fulfil their duties under the Children Act should be penalised.

The report also wants the Government to update homeless figures regularly and change the benefits system to give 18 year-olds increased allowances.

Andreas Whittam-Smith said: 'Most of the youngsters are on the street because of conflict at home, and feel they cannot go back.

'Yet they are confronted with jobs with low pay and state benefits which are sub-standard.

'It is time to get across the message. Homelessness makes no sense, socially or economically.'

Case studies

Mark, 25, and Mike, 21, Manchester

Brothers Mark and Mike Morley have been homeless since their teens.

They have spent their adult lives in and out of council care, custody and temporary accommodation.

'We can't go home because there's no space and Mum is ill,' says Mark. 'Every now and then we have to move on from temporary homes and end up on the streets. It's horrible – you have to sleep with one eye open in case you get done in.'

Both Mark and Mike are on methadone to fight heroin addiction brought on by 'sheer boredom and depression'.

Mark was put into care at 14. At 17 he got three months for theft, and he spent the next five years in and out of custody.

Mike left school at 14 and also went into care. At 16 social services placed him in a half-way house.

'Older lads used to call round and offer me pot,' says Mike. 'I also got heavily into amphetamines. They bullied me into burgling. They said I wouldn't go to jail because I was too young, but I was scared. It was definitely no adventure.'

Neither brother has ever held down a full-time job. Each earns a few pounds a week selling *The Big Issue*.

'It's depressing,' says Mark. 'Last week a lad grabbed all my *Big Issue's* and threw them across the road. It's the only way I can get money to live and then someone does that to you.'

Mike would like to be a fireman. Mark dreams of a career in the Army. But, says Mike: 'We'll never get to do those things now. We struggle just trying to survive.'

Sharon, 18, London

When Sharon Thomas was kicked out of the family home by the father she loved she was devastated.

The bust-up came after a clash with the lodger. Dad took the lodger's side. Sharon's mother had left home three years earlier and Sharon, 18, joined the ranks of the homeless.

'I had no idea where to go so I walked up and down the Old Kent Road,' she says. 'From there I headed to the West End, staying awake all night.'

The next day Sharon went to the Centrepoint hostel in London's Soho.

After five days she was referred to a comfortable, women-only hostel where she can stay for three months.

'All this moving around is pretty hard, but it seems you have no choice. I hope to start college when I'm settled,' she says.

Sharon, who passed her A-levels in the summer, hopes to go to university when she has sorted herself out.

'The overnight-stay hostels can be pretty horrible,' she says.

'They're clean but still stink and you're likely to get bitten by bugs. You have to be out by 9am and back in by 8pm, so it's pretty grim.

'I was lucky to find somewhere better after five nights.

'Everything the Government does is designed to force homeless young people to go back to their parents' house. But they don't understand.

'It's not my fault I'm homeless, I've been trying to talk to my dad but he's changed the phone number. There's no way home for me.'

Emma, 18, Bristol

Emma Lister was thrown out of her family home along with her twin brother Andrew when they were 15.

Today she lives on the streets of Bristol, begging for food and dodging police and pimps.

She says: 'My mother was studying for a degree and I don't think she could be bothered with us. I turned up on my dad's doorstep, but he sent me back to London. For a while Andrew and I slept on the streets together, but I haven't seen him in three years.'

Emma had a room in a private hostel, but the landlord threw her out when she fell behind with the rent.

She says: 'All the blankets were flea-ridden. In the squat I was in before it was even worse. There were loads of druggies, and they'd leave needles all over the place.

'I'm not into drugs or alcohol. I spend my money on food.

'It's often very dangerous being a woman on the streets. This pimp wanted me to go on the game and when I refused he kicked me in the ribs and stole my money.

'The police fined me £30 for begging. I couldn't pay, and was sent to prison for 14 days. It was awful.

'They make you work from six in the morning to seven at night for 50p a day.'

Now Emma has been given some hope. She says: 'I've been told I can go to college to study hairdressing. Hopefully I'll get a grant, so I can get somewhere to live.

All I want is a place of my own.'

Major problems

Range of problems experienced by residents of St Mungo's put forward for care assessments under Community Care arrangements.

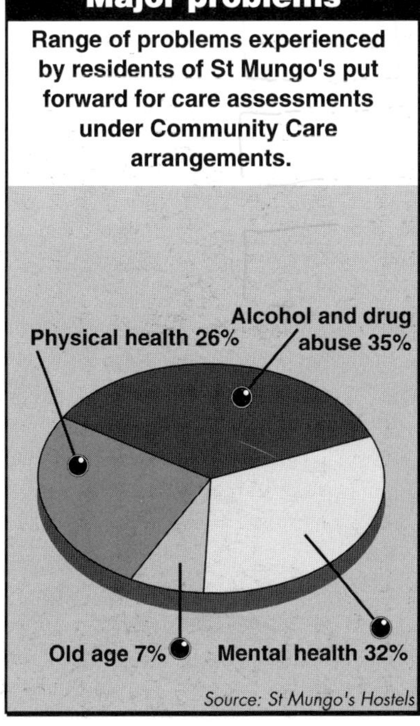

Source: St Mungo's Hostels

Paul, 19, Cheltenham

Paul Gibbard was full of bravado when his stepfather threw him out of the family home at the age of 15.

It would be easy, he told himself, as he set off down the road with a rucksack on his back. Get a job, get a flat, no problem.

Instead, Paul found himself in a nightmarish world of drugs and violence in which he was assaulted, robbed and exploited.

Between stays at horrifying hostels, he slept on park benches. He was often hungry, always frightened, sometimes suicidal.

After Paul's stepfather showed him the door, a homelessness project in Cheltenham, Glos, put him up in a seedy, grimy 'hotel' populated by thieves and drug addicts.

'I was too scared to go to bed. One 42-year-old guy there was a heroin addict and a psycho and said he was HIV-positive,' says Paul.

'He took me to a place he said was better, but it was worse.

'There were needles on the bathroom floor. This guy would come in steaming and smash my room up. Once he slammed me up against the wall, punched me, threatened me with an iron bar then chased me down the street.'

Today, Paul works as a volunteer for the Gloucestershire Forum For Young Single Homeless. He lives in a bedsit and has a baby son.

He says: 'I have had three nervous breakdowns. But each time I hit rock bottom I thought – this is it, I have to do something to get out.'

Homelessness in England

The facts

Level of homelessness in England

- In 1995 125,640 households were accepted as homeless by councils in England. This figure includes 4,830 households which were found to be 'intentionally homeless'. Local authorities have a very limited duty to accommodate intentionally homeless households.

- Shelter estimates that this represents about 360,000 individuals.

- In the first half of 1996 59,960 households were accepted as homeless by councils in England.

- Homelessness is a national problem. In 1995 nearly 78 per cent of households accepted as homeless were outside London.

- These figures are the tip of a very large iceberg because they only include those homeless households defined as being in 'priority need' for rehousing. This does not, for example, include the majority of single homeless people.

Thousands of single homeless people in England

- There are no comprehensive statistics for single homelessness nationally. In 1995 Single Homelessness in London (SHIL) estimated that there are about 45,000 single people in hostels, squats, short life housing, bed-and-breakfast hotels or sleeping out in London. In addition it is estimated that there are between 32,000 and 56,000 single 'hidden homeless' people in London, living in other people's houses or in overcrowded conditions.

- The 1991 Census recorded 2,674 people sleeping rough in 447 sites in England. This may not represent the actual figure because of the difficulty in counting less visible homeless people and those moving in and out of temporary accommo-dation.

Other vulnerable groups

- The London Research Centre estimated that in 1994 people from ethnic minorities represented 49 per cent of those accepted as homeless by London authorities.

- According to a Government survey in 1993 almost half of single homeless women in bed-and-breakfast hotels and hostels were from black or other ethnic minority groups.

- 7,250 households were accepted as homeless owing to mental illness of one of the household members during 1995. This represents an increase of 53 per cent since 1991.

- Recent Government research showed that 42 per cent of homeless applicants were under 25 years-old.

Temporary accommodation

- Being accepted as homeless is by no means the end of the story. Many homeless families are placed in inadequate temporary accommodation, such as bed-and-breakfast hotels, where they may stay for periods ranging from several months to years.

- At the end of June 1996 there were 43,800 families living in temporary accommodation in England. This total does not include the 9,310 households who were 'homeless at home' (households who continue to remain in their current accommodation while a more permanent home is found).

- The use of temporary accommodation in England has decreased by about 4.3 per cent since

September 1995, but it is still almost three times higher than ten years ago.

Bed-and-breakfast hotels

- The use of bed-and-breakfast hotels has decreased dramatically since the peak in 1991 when up to 13,500 families were living in this type of accommodation.
- At the end of June 1996 a total of 4,480 households were living in bed-and-breakfast hotels in England. Shelter estimates that this represents about 12,860 individuals, of whom about 5,000 are children.

Homelessness due to repossessions

- According to the Council of Mortgage Lenders a total of 49,410 properties were taken into possession in 1995 in the United Kingdom.
- At the end of 1995 a total of 389,780 home owners were in mortgage arrears of three months or more.

- In 1995 a total of 75,258 possession orders were made against home owners in England and Wales.

Homelessness costs

- In 1994/95 the total gross cost to local authorities in England of providing temporary accommodation for homeless households was over £260 million. Over £52 million of this total was spent on providing bed and breakfast accommodation.
- The Standing Conference on Public Health estimates that people in poor housing use the National Health Service 50 per cent more than average and that the cost to the NHS of poor living conditions is £2 billion a year.

Shelter believes:

- A decent, safe, secure and affordable home is a basic human right.
- Homelessness and poor housing cost in wasted resources and wasted lives.
- At least 100,000 additional affordable homes to rent each year are required to meet housing need.

Young homeless people

A compilation of information and research on young homeless people in Scotland

- In the year 1994/95 10,200 single young people aged between 16 and 25 applied for help under the homeless persons legislation.[1]
- This is likely to be an underestimate of the true figures since many young people will not apply to councils for help because they do not believe the council can help them.
- Many councils do not consider young people to be 'in priority need'. 20 out of the former 56 Scottish district or islands councils in 1992 automatically considered homeless 16 and 17 year-olds 'vulnerable' and therefore a priority; eight did the same for 18 year olds; two for 19-21 year-olds and only one for young people aged 22–25.[2]
- In 1994/95 8% or 3,300 of total homeless applicants in Scotland were 16 or 17 years old. 16.5% (6,900) of applicants were aged 18–24.[1]

- SCSH research suggests around two-thirds of young homeless people have experienced physical, sexual or emotional abuse.[3]
- Around 220 young people are referred to emergency hostel accommodation in Scotland each month. Only one in five can be admitted, usually because there are no free beds.[4]

References

1 *Scottish Office Statistical Bulletin* HSG 1996/3
2 *Some Change – Some Chance!* Shelter (Scotland) 1993
3 *Young People in and out of the Housing Market* 1993 SCSH/Edinburgh University Centre for Educational Sociology
4 *No Place Called Home* Shelter/SCSH 1994

Hearing young people

Information from the National Housing Federation

This paper, published to mark Youth Homelessness Week, is the first of a regular series of housing research summaries to be circulated with *Agenda* magazine. It sets out the results of a survey commissioned by the National Inquiry Into Preventing Youth Homelessness. Carried out in the summer of 1995, the research offers an important insight into how homeless young people view their own situation.

Introduction

Many of the young people interviewed for this report felt that being homeless was in some ways better than the life that the community, in its various guises, had offered them.

This key finding has implications for the whole of society, and particularly for statutory agencies and government. Young people do not choose to be homeless, but they often prefer it to what they left behind.

Many of the young people interviewed were in unstable or very temporary living conditions, if not sleeping rough. Their previous accommodation had been no more permanent, and they had often left their last situation to try to improve their living conditions.

But young people do not always view their experience of homelessness as a downward slide. The situation is more complex, with movement between different levels of impermanent or unsuitable accommodation, and often in and out of actual homelessness.

A young person's experience will often include both positive and negative elements. The positive is the new-found independence, the negative the harsh reality of rough sleeping, and the likelihood of being subjected to violence and abuse as well as the dangers of being drawn into prostitution, crime and drugs and alcohol.

It is not 'leaving care', or 'running away from home', that causes youth homelessness. It is a result of interacting social and economic factors, mainly connected with an apparent breakdown of the ways in which young people make the transition from dependence to independence.

Experiencing homelessness

There is little consensus as to what constitutes homelessness. It is much more than just street homeless or rooflessness. Young people tend to define homelessness as including living in a bed and breakfast, staying on friends' floors etc. Travellers have a different perspective. Whilst they are not always in a situation they prefer, they do not necessarily define themselves as being homeless. They are leading 'an alternative life-style' and belong to a 'travelling community'. The grievances they have are often about evictions from squatted premises and police harassment.

Rough sleeping

In rural areas such as Cornwall young people are likely to sleep out of sight, in caves or barns. The definition of rough sleeping needs to be more flexible to incorporate squatting in more derelict buildings and may be usefully extended to other forms of very temporary unsuitable situations. Research has shown that women and black homeless people tend not to sleep rough, as they fear additional harassment on the street due to their sex or colour. 69% of the interviewees had slept rough at some point whilst they had been homeless.

Many academics caution against the concept of a 'homeless career', with a downward spiral ending in rough sleeping. Hudson and Liddiard (1994) acknowledge these reservations but still distinguish an early, middle and late phase in homelessness:

Early phase

When respondents leave home or care they use a range of accommodation strategies. They often become homeless after being evicted from this first accommodation.

Many people may have to leave home or care in a crisis. After a short stay at friends or relatives they either move home or get a bedsit. They may sleep rough very short-term at this stage.

Middle phase

Young people who fail to return home or maintain secure accommodation at this point are likely to move into the middle phase. Types of accommodation use may change to hostels or in a smaller percentage of cases, to youth residential projects. Squatting may be an option and sleeping rough can be for longer periods of time. It becomes more difficult to retain employment and to move back into more secure accommodation.

Late phase

By this phase young people could be sleeping rough for long periods and also using the more traditional hostels and squats. At this point they are often seen as being too problematic for many services to deal with.

From the research we see that the long-term homeless adopt different accommodation strategies to the newly homeless. However, our research highlighted a more complex and fluid picture, where people move in and out of homelessness, and between the three stages.

The view from the street

In this section we are interested in the way young people describe and interpret their homelessness. Using the theories from Hudson and Liddiard (1994), it was apparent that the young people we spoke to did not always view their homelessness as a 'downward process'.

Some young people saw their situation as a learning process; an experience of life.

'It's a challenge.'

' . . . the ability to be able to live and survive in that environment . . .'

The lifestyle gave them more freedom of choice and space. It gave them the ability to live the life they choose.

'You can do what the hell you want when you've got freedom.'

'I don't see it as a problem. I move about, enjoy myself; live a bit.'

'I like the freedom and peace of mind.'

An important part of the experience was meeting people and making some good friends.

'I've made so many really good friends.'

'The people I mix with are always happy.'

'Rich people see buskers being happier than they are and they don't like it.'

They feel positive about their greater independence and for some their situation is better than the one they left.

Negative experience

This is tempered by some harsh realities:

' . . . so used to dossing around it becomes natural . . .'

' . . . felt like giving in . . .'

Poverty

Severe poverty and lack of basic food and clothing were commonly mentioned. Ill-health, the cold, and starvation are extreme consequences of poverty, which many of the young people had at some point experienced.

Other people

Many of the young people spoke of the negative attitudes of passers-by,

especially if they were begging or busking.

' . . . people look down on you . . .'

' . . . they call you a lazy bum.'

Throw-away remarks and aggressive comments from passers-by are seen as demeaning and threatening.

Depression

Many of the young homeless were seriously depressed:

'I cut up my arms and legs as I was so depressed.'

Prostitution

More homeless young gay men turned to prostitution than young women interviewed. This greatly increased their income, and they would begin to rely on it, but it also left them vulnerable to the possibility of rape or violence. They would occasionally have to fight for their money, and fight against attempted rape and violence. For the women interviewed, prostitution was more of a 'one-off'.

Drugs and friends dying

Whilst many young homeless do not take drugs regularly there is a debate as to the 'cause and effect' of drug taking and youth homelessness.

'Seeing friends die . . .'

' . . . a few near misses myself.'

Violence and abuse

Most of the homeless young people had experienced violence and abuse in some form:

- Passers-by and violence especially when busking and begging.
- Young women running from violence or abuse in their family home, or from their partners.
- Women were likely to have experienced some form of violence or sexual harassment if they were sleeping rough.

' . . . being asleep and waking up to find someone's hands down your trousers.' (young woman)

Two young gay men had experienced harassment, in flats they had been resettled into by the council, and others were subjected to harassment and violence in hostels due to their sexuality.

'I was kicked in the face and knocked out for being gay.'

Staff at some hostels were seen as anti-gay. Centrepoint in London was mentioned as one of the most sympathetic to gay issues.

• The above is an extract from *Research Agenda*, published by Agenda, National Housing Federation. See page 39 for address details.

The Crisis factsheet

The causes of homelessness

Housing

Since the mid-1970s public expenditure on housing has fallen. The number of council homes built over the last ten years has been insufficient to replace those sold to council tenants under the 'right to buy' scheme. This has contributed to the increase of homeless people, and also forced many people to live in unsuitable accommodation. This may include private rented and bed-and-breakfast accommodation. Many of these are 'houses in multiple occupation' (HMOs) where some of the worst living conditions may be found. Unemployment and redution of benefits (especially amongst young people) have compounded the problem. There are also many empty properties (public and private) that are not made available to people in need of accommodation. Recent legislation has introduced changes to benefits for people under 25, which may force young people into poor-quality, dangerous accommodation, or onto the streets.

Some statistics

- 2,600 local housing units were built in 1993; 69,605 were built in 1973. *Department of the Environment (DoE) Housing Data & Statistics 1996.*
- 804,000 properties registered as empty in England. *Department of the Environment (DoE) April 1995.*
- 130,000 mortgage borrowers in Britain are at risk of repossession. *Shelter 1995.*
- One in four homeless people has served in the forces (excluding National Service). *Crisis 1994.*
- 150,000 extra homes are needed in the UK. *National Housing Federation (NHF) 1995.*
- 70,000 local authority vacant properties were recorded in April 1996. *Department of the Environment (DoE) October 1996.*
- 45,000 single people are currently living in hostels, squats, short life housing, bed and breakfasts or sleeping rough in London. *Single Homeless in London (SHIL) 1995.*

Young people

Research from Centrepoint has shown an increase in the number of young homeless people. Contributory factors include reduction of benefits for 16 and 17 year-olds, which transfers the financial burden from the state to parents who may already be struggling. This may result in the child having to leave home. Young people may also have no alternative but to leave home due to intolerable conditions, eg violent or sexual abuse. Young people leaving care are in danger of becoming homeless if they do not receive proper support. Lack of affordable accommodation and unemployment add to the problem.

Some statistics

- One in four people who beg, slept on the street before the age of 16. *Crisis 1994.*
- 32% of young people seen between April 95 and March 96 were between 16 and 17 years of age. *Centrepoint 1996.*
- 25% of young people seen between April 95 and March 96 had just left care. *Centrepoint 1996.*
- Every year, Centrepoint sees around 200 children who have run away from either home or care. *Centrepoint 1996.*

Mental health

Mental health problems can be both a cause and a result of homelessness. A contributory factor to this problem is the failure to shift resources from hospitals to community-based services. The closure of psychiatric institutions has not been matched by the necessary increase in community based residential provision.

Some statistics

- Mental health problems were eight times as high among people in hostels and bed and breakfasts and eleven times as high among people sleeping rough when compared with the general population. *Centre for Housing Policy 1994.*
- Project workers at a central London hostel noticed a dramatic increase in the number of young people with mental health problems using their services. *National Housing Federation October 1996.*

Physical health

Homeless people are more likely to suffer bad physical health, due mainly to poor living conditions and inadequate diet, which can affect an individual's immune system. This is often compounded by problems in getting access to health services, or even attending to basic hygiene.

Some statistics

- One in 50 single homeless people in central London screened by Crisis had active tuberculosis. *Crisis 1995.*
- 37% of young homeless people using Centrepoint had experienced a deterioration in their health. *Centrepoint 1994.*
- Chronic chest or breathing problems were twice as high among people in hostels and B and Bs and three times as high among people sleeping rough when compared with the general population. *Centre for Housing Policy 1994.*
- Wounds, skin ulcers or other skin complaints were similar among people in hostels and B and Bs, twice as high among people using

day centres and three times as high among people using soup runs when compared with the general population. *Centre for Housing Policy 1994.*

Women

Whilst homelessness amongst women does exist, in many cases it remains 'hidden'. This means that they are not necessarily street homeless, but may be tolerating a dysfunctional relationship, or poor-quality housing, because of fear of leaving and lack of knowledge of alternatives. Women are also more likely to stay with friends or relatives, sometimes in overcrowded conditions, and may not even regard their situation as homelessness. Young women leaving care are particularly vulnerable. Unemploy-ment and lack of benefits for 16 and 17 year-old women add to the problem.

Some statistics

- The number of women using the Crisis WinterWatch shelters increased slightly from 13% (1995) to 16% (1996). *Crisis Winterwatch survey 1996.*
- 43% of women staying at Crisis WinterWatch shelters had become homeless as a result of a dispute with their partner compared to 40% in 1995. *Crisis WinterWatch survey 1996.*
- Over 50% of women contacting Women's Link between April 95 and March 96 had just left prison. *Women's Link October 1996.*
- 44% of women seeking advice from Women's Link were aged between 26 and 35 years. *Women's Link October 1996.*

Ethnic minorities

As with the situation for women, people from ethnic groups are often 'hidden homeless' tending to stay in overcrowded or inadequate accommodation rather than become visibly homeless. Many young people from ethnic backgrounds become homeless if their parents decide to return to their homeland. They may have a fear of using hostels and can suffer discrimination when trying to find permanent accommodation.

Some statistics

- Almost half of all women in hostels and B&Bs were from black or minority ethnic groups. Nearly a half of all the people from minority ethnic groups were under 25. *School of Sociology & Social Policy, University of Leeds 1996.*
- Centrepoint found that 44% of the 729 young people admitted to their hostels in 1993 defined themselves as black or mixed race. 51% of black hostel dwellers included in the survey were female. *Centrepoint 1996.*
- Young black people were less likely to have slept rough than their white counterparts (20% of young black people, 47% of young white people) and were also less likely to have ever used a squat (4% of young black people, 22% of young white people). *Centrepoint 1996.*

Elderly people

The proportion of people aged 75 and over is due to increase in the next 25 years. Elderly homeless people are particularly vulnerable, especially if they are street homeless. They may have become homeless in middle age and found it impossible to secure a permanent home, and may also be unaware of their rights or available sources of support. Elderly people who have accommodation often live in unsuitable or poor housing conditions.

Some statistics

- People aged 45 and over form 32% of people residing in hostels and B&Bs (as compared to 30% for people aged 16–25-years), 38% of those using day centres (as compared to 30% for people 16–25 years) and 35% of soup run users (as compared to 19% of people aged 16–25 years). *Department of the Environment (DoE) Anderson et al 1993.*
- Middle-aged and elderly men within the homeless community are particularly vulnerable to tuberculosis. *Crisis 1995.*
- 80% of street homeless people in London aged over 60 had been sleeping rough for five years or more. *Shelter 1993.*

Reasons for homelessness

Detailed analysis reveals that 40% of those officially homeless in Britain became so because parents, relatives or friends were no longer willing or able to accommodate them.

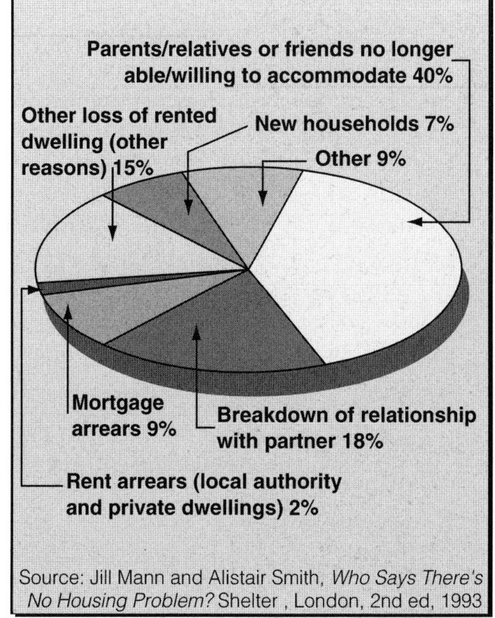

Source: Jill Mann and Alistair Smith, *Who Says There's No Housing Problem?* Shelter , London, 2nd ed, 1993

Alcohol and drugs

The experience of homelessness can lead to drink or drug dependency, although such dependency can also be a contributory factor to becoming homeless. Drink or drugs act as an anaesthetic blocking out the misery of homelessness, but they also add to the problems homeless people face such as bad diet and health, and can act as an obstacle to finding a solution to their homeless situation. Homeless heavy drinkers are a particularly vulnerable group, frequently subject to physical injury when intoxicated.

Some statistics

- 30% of single homeless people have problems with alcohol. *CHAR 1993.*
- One-third of people begging have a substance abuse problem. *Crisis 1994.*
- Currently it is estimated that there are 800 homeless heavy drinkers in Bristol, between 150 and 200 are under 25 years old. *ACAD 1996.*

Family homelessness

'We believe that the right to a secure home base is basic. For anyone, but particularly families, to be without a permanent home for any length of time can be a dehumanising experience. It is especially humiliating for parents when they cannot secure a proper home for their children.'
Bishop Ronald Bowlby (President CNHC) and Archbishop Derek Worlock (Vice-President CNHC), letter to Housing Minister, July 1994.

Homelessness in Britain

- Every working day, on average, more than 1,000 households apply to local councils for help on the grounds of homelessness.
- During the 1990s, well over a million households in Britain have been registered as homeless by local authorities. That means more than 3 million people – half of them children.
- Homelessness is a national problem affecting a large number of people and different kinds of area from inner cities to rural villages.
- Homelessness is not a passing phenomenon – it has been increasing and spreading for the past thirty years, but took a stronger hold in the 1980s and early 1990s.
- The critical problem is a shortage of affordable rented housing.

Homeless families' access to permanent housing

The 1977 Housing (Homeless Persons) Act placed a duty on local housing authorities to ensure that homeless people who are categorised as being in priority need and who are not intentionally homeless are provided with permanent accommodation. This duty was abolished in the 1996 Housing Act, and replaced with a much more limited duty to provide assistance with finding temporary accommodation. If the local authority considers that there is suitable alternative accommodation available locally (e.g. in the private rented sector), then it has no duty to provide housing of any kind.

A number of factors have made it increasingly difficult for local authorities to provide permanent housing for homeless people. Since 1977, the number of households accepted as homeless by local authorities in England has more than doubled: from 53,000 in 1978 to over 121,000 in 1995.

Acceptances represent between a half and a third of applications under the legislation. Of the 343,000 households who applied as homeless in 1992 in England, 148,250 were accepted as homeless. The proportion of households accepted is dropping as councils face greater pressure on their housing stock.

Council housing stock has diminished because of sales under the right to buy and the failure, owing to Government spending restrictions, to replace these houses. The Government's shift away from funding the building of new homes by councils and housing associations towards subsidising individual tenant rents via means-tested Housing Benefit has led to a yearly decline in social housing. The lack of homes for rent has meant that those who are accepted as homeless are housed for long periods in temporary, usually unsuitable accommodation while waiting for permanent housing.

Families' experience of homelessness: myth and reality – jumping the queue

The Department of the Environment introduced legislation at the end of 1995 to end local authorities' duty to provide homeless families with permanent housing. One of the main reasons the Department gave for this is that it considered it to be unfair to give homeless families automatic priority over others on the waiting list in the allocation of permanent council or housing association tenancies. It claimed that:

'*. . . this makes the homelessness route seem the more attractive way into subsidised housing for those wishing to be re-housed.*'

Yet, earlier research commissioned by the Department itself had found that people accepted by the local authority as homeless and living in temporary accommodation, far from being manipulative and calculating queue-jumpers, turn to the local council for assistance only in the last resort:

'A very common pattern of homelessness began with the breakdown of domestic arrangements, after which the respondent found alternative accommodation with friends or relations. It was only when this credit was exhausted, faced with shortages in the private rented sector and the prohibitive costs of ownership, that they approached the local authority. In this sense [homeless people] had pursued all the housing options available to them. They saw the local authority as a last resort, and a solution forced on them by what they saw as a shortage of affordable housing... The image of well-informed, demanding and undeserving people making unreasonable claims on the local authority is far from the picture revealed by the survey.' (*Living in temporary accommodation*, Department of the Environment, 1989).

Babies on benefit . . .

It is a popular myth often repeated in the media, that single parents and especially 'young, unmarried mothers' deliberately become pregnant to jump the housing queue.

No evidence has been produced to substantiate such allegations. Firstly, current legislation makes no differentiation between one-parent and two-parent families who become homeless. Secondly, reports published by the Department of the Environment itself show that:

- A majority of lone parents with young children who become homeless have experienced the breakdown of a marriage or other partnership.
- About half of them have previously had a permanent home of their own, either as tenants or, for a growing number, as house-buyers.
- The average age of lone parents in accommodation for the homeless is in the mid-to-late twenties, and a very small percentage are unmarried teenage girls.

The experience of homelessness

Homeless families' experience of homelessness, and the assistance they receive from local authorities, varies enormously not only in different parts of the country but also from council to council. Some councils still have sufficient housing available to them to be able to offer permanent accommodation immediately, although this is becoming increasingly rare. A survey in 1994 found that homeless households had to spend on average over 8 months in temporary accommodation before being provided with permanent housing.

The majority of councils have to provide some form of emergency or temporary accommodation. This itself can vary greatly, from short leases in council properties and council-run hostels, through women's refuges, voluntary-run hostels and privately owned property leased by the council to the worst-quality bed-and-breakfast hotels. In September 1996, almost 44,000 homeless households were being temporarily accommodated by local authorities in England. Figures produced by Shelter and the London Housing Unit show that in many instances the cost of using temporary accommodation is greater than that of providing permanent housing for homeless families (*Homes cost less than homelessness*, 1992).

Living in temporary accommodation

'It's unsettling; you just live with your bare necessities... Even though you've got a roof over your head, you haven't got a home.'

Living in temporary accommodation represents a miserable and unsettling experience for many families. There is a widely held view that the households that do get placed in temporary accommodation will normally survive without too much damage because it is only for a short period. For many the reality is different. Despite the term 'temporary' this is an existence which has to be endured for anything from a couple of weeks to four years, with little guarantee of what sort of housing they will be offered at the end of it. Among the consequences for individuals and families are:

- difficulty in making plans, due to uncertainty about the length of stay in temporary accommodation
- separation from friends and family networks
- difficulty in getting or keeping a job
- interrupted schooling and isolation from friends, for the children
- being cut off from cultural and religious links and supports
- difficulties in maintaining contact with the placing council's Homeless Persons Unit and social services, and the children's schools
- disruption of health care, and severance of contact with the family's GP and health visitor
- loss of voting rights
- lack of identification with the area in which the temporary accommodation is located.

Length of time on waiting list, by type of local authority and Department of the Environment region

Median years on list before being offered permanent accommodation

	All new tenants	Housed as statutory homeless	Housed from general waiting list
All new tenants	**1.0**	**0.7**	**1.2**
Type of authority			
London boroughs	1.0	1.0	1.8
Other metropolitan	0.8	0.4	1.1
Non-metropolitan	1.1	0.8	1.3
DoE region			
North	0.9	0.5	1.1
Midlands	0.9	0.6	1.2
London	1.0	1.0	1.8
South	1.2	0.9	2.0

Source: Routes into Local Authority Housing, DoE, 1994, table 4.30

Households temporarily accommodated by local authorities at the end of September 1996

	In B&B hotels	In hostels (inc women's refuges)	In other temporary accommodation	Total
England	4550	10440	28860	43810
North East	90	210	130	430
Yorkshire & Humberside	110	570	520	1200
East Midlands	70	700	830	1600
East Anglia/Eastern	110	980	1790	2880
South East (excluding London)	710	1830	4350	6890
London	2900	3700	18440	25040
South West	260	670	1620	2550
West Midlands	90	420	600	1110
North West	210	1320	580	2110

Source: Department of the Environment quarterly homelessness statistics, third quarter 1996

Homeless families 'still torn apart'

James Meikle on a law that is not working

'Families with children in care can be caught in a vicious circle. Without a home, they cannot get their children back. Until their children return, the council will not provide them with a home.'

Families are being torn apart by homelessness despite legislation that was meant to stop parents and children being parted, the housing charity Shelter said yesterday.

Thousands of people of all ages were suffering stress, depression, health and education problems because authorities either did not realise they were in trouble or would not give them priority help.

Shelter said one in 12 applicants for emergency rehousing were from split households and one in seven on normal housing waiting lists were in a similar position.

Many authorities did not even realise homeless applicants were from families that lived apart. Even when they did, they rejected two-thirds of cases, Shelter said in a report to mark its 30th birthday.

The report, *Divided Lives*, comes 30 years after *Cathy Come Home*, the BBC television drama that helped fuel the campaign to stop homeless families being broken up. Shelter said its advice centres saw at least 1,000 split families a year. But there were many more, hidden from statistics, staying with parents, relatives and friends.

Homelessness legislation since 1977 has meant families should not be forced to live apart if they do not have a home. But low incomes usually meant families could not afford to buy or rent good-quality accommodation. 'If housing and social services departments do not work together, families with children in care can be caught in a vicious circle. Without a home, they cannot get their children back. Until their children return, the council will not provide them with a home.' Shelter has condemned Government for removing homeless people from priority for permanent accommodation under the 1996 Housing Act. It called for a wider definition of split households so that people needing to live with a carer, to prevent them going into residential homes, and lesbians and gay men could be helped with suitable homes.

'200 homeowners a day still lost their homes to repossession, 2,000 households a week were given shelter because they had nowhere to live'

Chris Holmes, Shelter's director, said there had been improvements since 1966.

'Many of the worst slums have been replaced. Homeless families' children are not routinely taken into care although there are still threats of it.' But 200 homeowners a day still lost their homes to repossession, 2,000 households a week were given shelter because they had nowhere to live, young people were having difficulty in finding homes and too many people were still living rough on the streets.

The Department for the Environment rejected suggestions from Shelter that its figures showed split households up from 1,331 to 1,954 between 1994 and 1995.

'They don't show an increase in families being forced to live apart.

The problem

In 1994, 146,119 households (families) in Great Britain were accepted as homeless by local authorities. This is estimated to represent about 419,400 individuals.

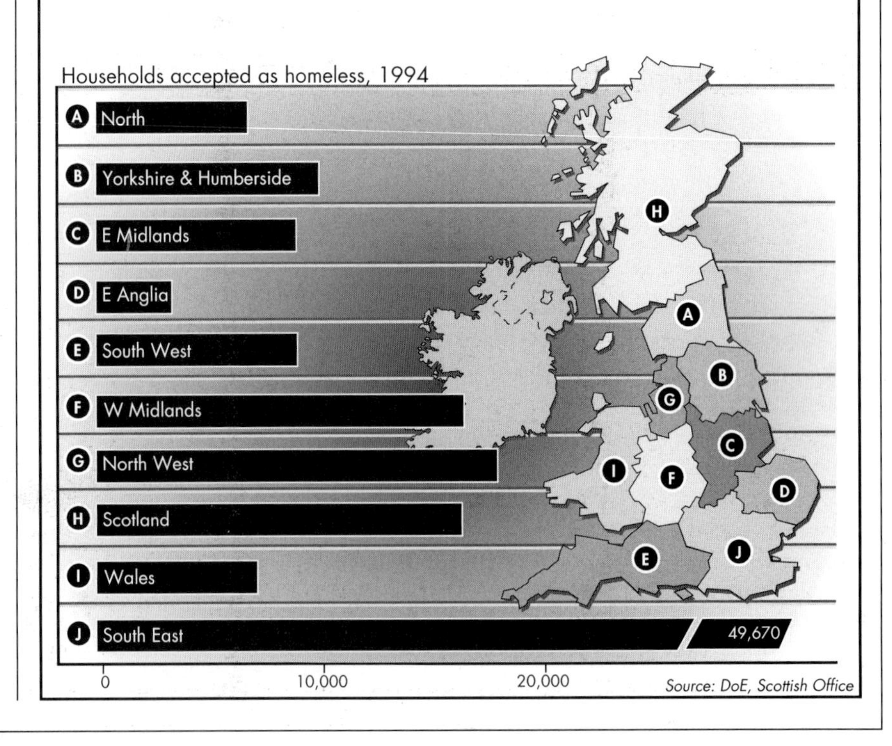

They reflect the normal splits – for instance, a pregnant woman moving away to live with her partner.'

The Langleys – Chris, Anne, Paula, 17, and Gareth, 9

They left their rented home when the landlady wanted to turn it into single rooms. Slough borough council, Berkshire, said they were intentionally homeless and did not qualify for immediate rehousing.

They went into a hostel, Chris lost his job putting up For Sale signs outside private houses. They moved out. Shelter helped find them bed-and-breakfast accommodation, all four in one room; they had problems getting benefit and Paula moved out. The authorities frown on a young woman sharing such cramped accommodation with her father.

After two months staying with friends she was back. She had wanted her freedom and space. Her mother missed her. Berkshire social services offered the family half the deposit needed to find rented accommodation and warned that if it failed to do so, Gareth, an asthmatic, might be taken into care, while Paula was capable of finding accommodation on her own.

With Shelter's help, they found a place to live. The lease runs out in November. Anne bursts into tears when she tells how she was afraid the family would be split up. 'We are reasonably happy at the moment but unless we find another tenancy, and hopefully the council will give us a tenancy, but I can't take any more.'

Marking time
30 years of homelessness

Temporary accommodation

1966: England and Wales: 13,031 individuals including 2,558 families

1996: England: 43,330 households
Direct comparisons difficult because of new definitions.

Unfit homes

1967: England and Wales: 1.8 million

1995: England: 1.5 million

House Building

1966: England: 330,120, of which 187,885 private

1995: England: 155,475, of which 123,590 private

Accepted as homeless for emergency housing

1995: England: 125,640 households
No comparable figures in 1966

The Halls – David, Susan, James, 16, Sean, 15, Daniel, 4, and Sarah, 2

David, after some years doing seasonal catering work in Plymouth, Devon, went on a training course for six weeks and tried to find more regular work. Susan's sister said there was a lot around Chippenham, Wiltshire. David had some interviews for jobs, but, said Susan, there was no way they could live apart.

David checked with the council, who were positive. They had family in the area, they did not want to be split up, he was working, there was a good chance they would get a house. He got a low-paid job in a restaurant near Chippenham early in June. North Wiltshire refused his application under homeless legislation because Susan and the family were adequately housed in a privately rented home in Plymouth. They have gone onto a waiting list.

David last saw the family 4½ weeks ago. He makes few trips home in the old Volvo because he only has £20 to £25 a week left after paying for lodgings and living expenses. Most of it he sends home. 'He has thought of giving up the job,' said Susan. 'But if he does he loses benefits for six months. We can't go forward and we can't go back.'

If the family knew when they might get a home, she could negotiate payments for bills in Plymouth. They have family credit but there is only about £9 a week for Susan to feed the children. 'All I want is a home with my husband in Wiltshire. It is emotionally draining living like this, having to explain why their father is not there. Daniel asks every night when Dad is coming home. You just feel so insecure.'

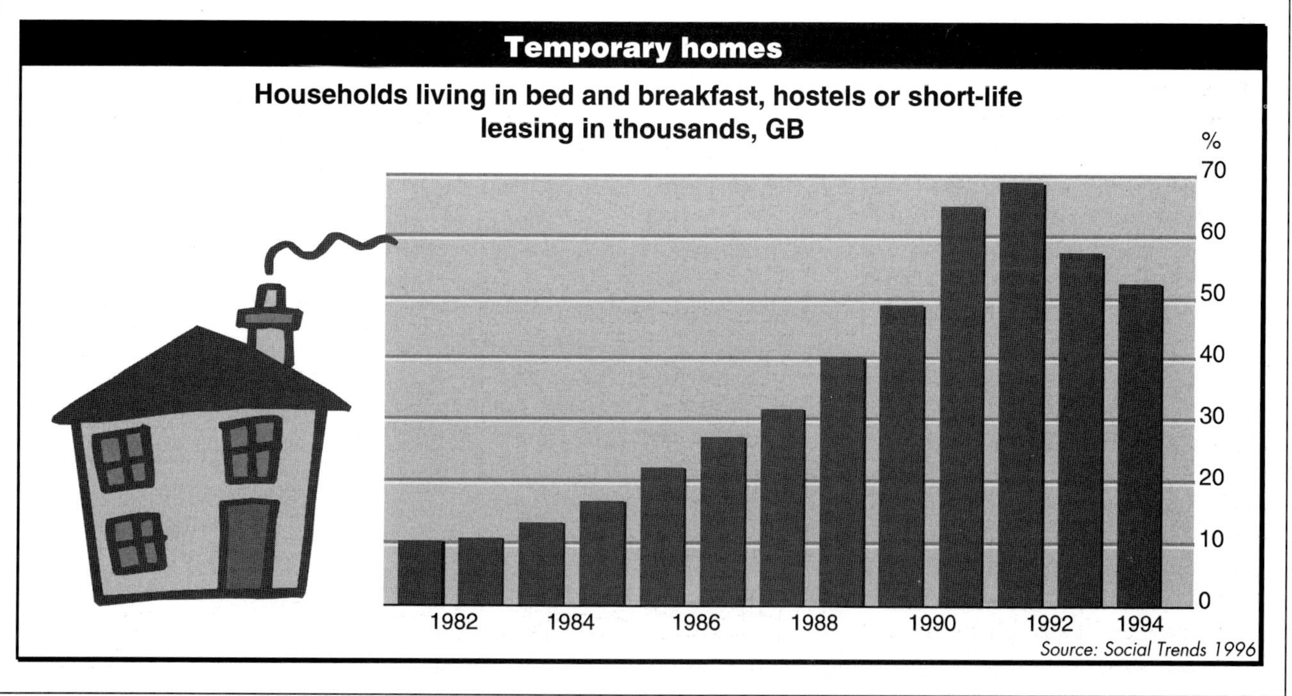

Homing instincts

It's even tougher for women in hostels, reports Esme Madill

Who is most likely to be homeless? Did you think immediately of an old man with a bottle in his hand? In fact, four in ten homeless people living in hostels are women. Among the young homeless, the proportion is even higher: two-thirds of hostel residents under 24 are women.

There is no official count of black homelessness but a recent straw poll of six central London hostels and nightshelters suggests 45 per cent of young women in hostels are black. If the statistics are inadequate, it is because women's homelessness has failed to excite much interest.

Figures badly underestimate the problem. What is notable about women's homelessness is its invisibility. Women are even more reluctant than men to take to the streets: the streets hold particular threats for women. Hostels and nightshelters can also be dangerous. Many house both sexes and can be frightening places. Women who have recently been made homeless and those with mental health problems are especially at risk. Black women speak of encountering racism from staff as well as residents. Lesbians tell of verbal and physical abuse.

Faced with all this, not surprisingly, many women opt for the devil they know, which frequently means remaining at home with a violent partner or parent. We do know that of those young women who are street homeless or living in hostels, four in ten are there because they have fled sexual assault at home. Even those brave enough to leave home can find that the few unattractive options available force them into another violent or abusive relationship. An older man who knows the ropes can initially offer protection and security of a kind.

Clearly, at the very least women need safe, affordable housing. However, local authorities have no duty to house single homeless women unless they are pregnant, over 60 years of age, or are deemed to be in sufficiently poor physical or mental health. Even if there were enough homes, homelessness is more than just the lack of a roof. Many women who find themselves homeless have recently been severely distressed: they may have left an abusive partner or parent, or fled a country where they were persecuted and witnessed torture.

There are very few women-only hostels which offer support as well as the chance to move into a home of your own

Homeless people are more likely than others to have lost a parent through death or divorce. Many will have come from local authority care or insecure housing where they faced harassment from neighbours or other tenants over race, ethnicity or sexuality. All this compounds the problems of homelessness and leaves women in need of more than just a place to sleep.

Some women will never have had a home of their own and will have left local authority care or their family home without the practical or emotional skills necessary to live alone. Others will have mental or physical health problems which make it harder to live independently. If you set up your first home with a group of fellow students in college, or with the support of family and friends, coupled with a steady income, there will be second-hand furniture, loans and advice. You can afford to learn through trial and error.

For others, life is very different. It is not easy to negotiate with the electricity suppliers if you have no deposit and need to get a key meter fitted, but don't know who to contact and are having to call from a phone box with little change.

If you are refused a Community Care Grant, which frequently occurs, you will have no money to purchase essentials such as a bed or a cooker. It takes a great deal of time and energy to learn to cook, clean, budget, deal with minor repairs and arrange paying bills. On a weekly income of £46 (or £28 for those under 18), there is no room for mistakes. Those who have to move into their own flat or bedsit without preparation and support are more likely to get into difficulties. If no help is available they could end up homeless again.

There are very few women-only hostels which offer support as well as the chance to move into a home of your own. They cannot begin to cope with the large numbers of homeless women needing their help. Homeless Action is one solution. It provides good-standard, safe, secure accommodation to single homeless women or women threatened with homelessness. Women who approach it live in small shared houses, or one of a few self-contained flats. Where possible, they are rehoused in their own local authority or housing association flats. The key to its success is commitment to providing support which caters to a woman's needs to enable her to gain the confidence, skills and support necessary to live in her own home and fulfil her potential.

• Esme Madill is research and development manager at Homeless Action.

Dependency with no know-how

To be elderly and homeless is to be doubly vulnerable

By Michael Simmons

Homelessness has existed at least since Roman times, but no one has yet been able to measure the size of the problem. Informed guesses have been made about how many people are roofless, and central and local government have framed policies accordingly, but pressure groups and charities working with the homeless routinely feel they underestimate the problem.

This is particularly the case with the elderly homeless, where measurement is almost impossible. However, it has been estimated that of the 160,000 'households' (more than 400,000 individuals) accepted as statutorily homeless by local authorities in England and Wales last year, over 6 per cent were over 60. The homeless charity St Mungo's, which works closely with the elderly, says about one in ten of those entering its hostels over the last four years have been over 55, with about 40 per cent of the total coming in off the streets.

Many of the elderly are mentally ill and may have severe drink problems. Often they have been living on the streets for years, though others may arrive in later life, following the death of a spouse or other close relative. Although violence on the streets is not uncommon, these people paradoxically feel safer on the streets because they feel less paranoid there. Some are so confused they don't know their age or date of birth.

Biographical details are hard to come by because the elderly hide away, or are evasive or proud when approached. Specialists who have worked with them and researchers who have approached them, however, broadly agree they are probably the most vulnerable of all the 'casualties' now in the hands of the welfare state, caught up in a dependency culture when they may lack the know-how even to be dependent. Help the Aged says at least a million old people are currently failing to claim the income support to which they are entitled, a figure which will increase in the medium term as pension provision declines. In conjunction with another homeless charity, Crisis, which says one in six of the homeless is over 60, Help the Aged has recently commissioned research, to be published early next year, into the incidence of homelessness among the elderly, their distinctive needs and what can be done to resettle and rehabilitate the people concerned.

The researcher is Maureen Crane, a former psychiatric nurse now attached to the Department of Health Care for Elderly People at Sheffield University. She has spent hundreds of hours interviewing the homeless elderly in London, Sheffield, Leeds and Manchester. Often this has meant seeking them out in backstreet hiding places, away from other people.

Many of those she has met, Crane has found, have never even used homeless 'facilities', including purpose-made drop-in centres. Some,

once she has found them, have been too ill or unwilling, for various reasons, to be interviewed.

Crane describes one of the people she did meet: 'Miss D., aged 68, was born and brought up in Manchester ... She slept on her own in an isolated area ... She was wearing many layers of dirty clothing; her hygiene was very poor; her face and hands were very dirty ... She had a supermarket trolley full of old bags and other rubbish.'

But the plight of Miss D., says Crane, is by no means unique. George B., aged 74, who is frail and vulnerable and has a drink problem, may count himself luckier than Miss D. He is now being looked after in a special home for the elderly on the Lancashire coast, with fees of £200 a week being paid out of emergency charitable reserves held by Bondway Housing Association, London.

Although George hailed originally from Portsmouth, the city wouldn't take him on or pay for his accommodation. Nor would the London borough of Lambeth, where he had most recently been living; which is why he is in Lancashire and far away from the few connections he has left in his life. 'It is outrageous,' says Tony Walters, at Bondway, 'that local authorities are so reluctant to pay for this accommodation.' The circumstances of George B. are also by no means unique, Walters adds. He gets frightened when he is in a large dormitory, where violence may break out, and he dislikes the noise and lack of privacy which characterises many hostels. He is not alone in this.

The Help the Aged/Crisis research project highlights the difficulties of the subject. Definitions of homelessness will – yet again – be attempted and evidence sought of the extent of the problem. There will be scrutiny of the 'pathways into homelessness' taken by old people, such as bereavement, breakdown of close relationships, work problems, mental illness and discharge from the army.

At Help the Aged, Caroline Welch says homelessness has for too long been regarded as a problem of young people. 'The elderly are especially vulnerable and damaged,' she says. 'The counselling they so badly need is that much more difficult and the chances of them getting a job are more remote. We intend setting up a new range of services to help them – when we have the facts.'

At Crisis, director Mark Scothern argues: 'Old people are at the most difficult times of their entire lives. If they are homeless and alone, their difficulties are that much greater.'

Scandal – time to act

Life on the streets

'I got mugged for £1.63 when I was in London. I was beaten with a golfing umbrella and in hospital for three days. It took the ambulance 45 minutes to come to me.'

(Kevin, homeless in Brighton)

If we become homeless, we can expect life to be extremely tough for us. Those interviewed were asked to list the worst elements based on their experience.

Worst feature of being homeless	Percentage
Physical assaults	17.5
Hypothermia and physical illness	10
Social isolation	9
Theft and loss of belongings	8
Break-up of family, loneliness	7
Rape/sexual exploitation	7
Sleeping rough	7
Humiliation, stigma	6
Police harassment	5.5
Hunger	5
Lack of money	4
Depression	4
Uncertainty: family, future	2.5
Being frightened, being helpless	2.5
Being driven to crime or prostitution	2
Not being able to wash or be clean	2
Unpleasantness of hostels	1
Lack of work, boredom	1
Other	5.5

The people in our study reported:

- Lots of physical and sexual assaults.
- Physical problems including hypothermia, muscular pains from sleeping rough and injuries resulting from assaults.
- Mental and physical health problems are understandably common amongst people who are homeless. There is a lack of out-reach community care support, and the general feelings of isolation can be devastating.
- Many respondents reported feelings of isolation, humiliation and depression.
- Being afraid, feeling helpless, loss of control over one's life and being pressured to take drugs are also highlighted.

• The above is an extract from *Scandal – Time to act*, published by The Methodist Association of Youth Clubs (MAYC). See page 39 for address details.

Sleeping rough

Information from Crisis

The number of rough sleepers who die during a year and their causes of death were researched through Coroner's Courts records (1 September 1995 to 31 August 1996). We explored what it is about being homeless that contributes to a much shorter life expectancy than the general population through in-depth interviews with 20 homeless people and 25 voluntary and statutory agencies and a literature review.

Key findings

Mortality

The number of rough sleeper deaths has remained at substantially the same level while the number of people counted on the streets on any one night has decreased:

- 74 deaths of rough sleepers were recorded in Coroner's Courts in London in the 1995/96 period when there was a central London head count of 365 rough sleepers, compared with 86 deaths in the 1991/92 period when there was a higher central London head count of 741
- this increased 'proportion' is likely to reflect more people sleeping rough but for shorter periods of time and/or the fact that the Government's Rough Sleepers Initiative is not yet helping many of the most vulnerable rough sleepers.

The life expectancy of someone who sleeps rough is 42 years, compared with the national average of 74 for men and 79 for women. The average was found to be 47 years in 1991/92. The decrease is likely to reflect the rising number of young homeless people.

- The average age of death for a rough sleeper dying from natural causes is 46 years.

- Rough sleepers are 35 times more likely to kill themselves than the general population.
- Rough sleepers are four times more likely to die from unnatural causes such as accidents, assaults, murder, drug or alcohol poisoning.
- The mortality rate for homeless people is between 3.8 and 5.6 times that of the general population.

Underlying causes

- Keeping warm and finding something to eat are often the priority for homeless people so that health is not prioritised.
- Alcohol and drug misuse affect some homeless people, but by no means the majority. Alcohol and drugs are also used as a form of self-medication when dealing with physical and mental pain. For some, death is therefore linked with alcohol and drugs, but on the whole it is the harsh setting and lifestyle that contributes to an early death.
- Mental illness and disorders are common and some would say go with the territory, almost as if to adapt to being homeless is to develop a mental health problem. This impacts on an individual's ability to look after themselves and can result in extreme self-neglect. Suicidal thoughts and tendencies as well as self-cutting are also present in a significant minority.
- As well as suffering more severe health problems, homeless people experience specific difficulties in accessing the health care they need. Further to this, someone who is homeless is more likely to seek help only when their condition is acute or severe.

Other issues

- The theory of the 'three-week rule', first put forward in *Sick to death of homelessness*, which describes the period during which people rapidly adapt to homelessness in order to survive, and after which it is more difficult to integrate back into mainstream society, was generally supported by this research.
- Emergency cold-weather shelters help to save lives. While there were slightly more deaths during the winter months, the proportion was not substantially higher than for the general population. The lifesaving role of cold-weather shelters was cited in interviews with both agencies and homeless people.
- Homeless people often die alone and without a commemoration. Many die on the street and are found by passers-by – be they children, tourists or people going to work. Individuals are remembered at parish funerals where two or three people attend, with an allowance of £25 towards flowers.

• The above is an extract from *Still dying for a home*, published by Crisis. See page 39 for address details.

£4m shelters for rough sleepers

Lottery cash will aid charity's scheme to set up national chain of emergency refuges to help 1,500 homeless people a year by 1997

By James Meikle, Community Affairs Editor

A national chain of year-round emergency shelters for homeless people is launched today in an attempt to cut the numbers sleeping rough.

The housing charity Crisis plans to spend at least £4 million, including £487,000 in National Lottery funds, establishing 11 'open houses' by the autumn. The money will also cover running costs for three years.

Six more shelters are expected in 1997 as the network provides accommodation for about 1,500 people a year.

The move, for which funds will also be raised locally, coincides with an extension of the Government's programme to help rough sleepers outside central London.

Only Gloucester, Cambridge, and Basingstoke among the centres so far named for the Crisis plan coincide with 23 areas where the Department of the Environment is considering grants, having already promised aid in Bristol.

Housing minister David Curry will today open the Crisis project in Cambridge. Others in the first wave include Crawley, East Sussex, Doncaster, and Stevenage, Hertfordshire. Hull is the other city so far identified by Crisis.

The programme, which in many cases involves local voluntary groups, is designed to ensure consistent standards for helping street homeless, both with accommodation and back-up services from housing and medical advice to laundries. Demand for beds at some hostels has been so high that 'difficult' clients, including those with behavioural, drink, drug or mental health problems, have been turned away.

Some hostels are said to have such punitive rules that people prefer to stay sleeping out while other hostels have gained a reputation for having residents who are rough and violent.

Crisis and fellow charity Shelter already help local groups provide temporary winter shelters. A spot check covering 21 projects in February found 281 residents, 90 per cent of whom had previously slept rough.

Mark Scothern, Crisis director, said: 'Sleeping rough is damaging and degrading. Voluntary and statutory agencies must work together throughout the UK to provide all rough sleepers with a route off the streets.'

Summary comparison between 1991/92 and 1995/96

Suicide is still a major cause of death amongst rough sleepers. More people died from natural causes during 1995/96 than in 1991/92 and fewer from accidents and assaults. These differences are not statistically significant, whereas the similarities add considerable weight to our knowledge about the health risks of being homeless.

	1991/92	1995/96
Number of records of deaths	86	74
Male	82%	92%
Female	18%	8%
Average age	47	42

• *From* Still Dying for a Home, *published by Crisis.*

Are you 16 or 17 and homeless?

You might be entitled to help under the Children Act

Who from . . . ? Social Services

You must be joking. I want to get as far away from social services as possible. I'm not staying in a children's home.

That's OK – social services have to ask what you want and can help with hostels, supported lodgings or your own flat. Don't be put off asking for help because it's social services.

But I haven't been in care.
It doesn't matter. Under section 17 they have a duty to help you if you are in need, and to provide accommodation under section 20(3), if you are homeless, 16 or 17 and are a 'child in need' whose welfare is likely to be seriously prejudiced.

What does that mean?
If your emotional, physical or intellectual development is likely to be affected by your situation. Being homeless is bad for your health in lots of ways – you may not be able to sleep or eat well or get on with your life properly. Many people become homeless because of abuse or violence or being thrown out of home – in all these cases you are 'in need'.

I was in care when I was young for a while but returned home – do I come under this part of the Act?
Yes, section 20 is for anyone who needs help and is under 18.

I was in care after my 16th birthday – do I come under this part of the Act?
Yes, if you are under 18. You can also get help from social services under section 24 of the Act until you are 21.

Confused?
Get an adult you trust or an advice worker to help you. Don't forget, if you are homeless you are probably a child in need.

OK – so how do I get help under section 20 of the Act?

Step-by-step guide

1. If possible
Get help or advice before going to social services. Try to get an adult you trust to go with you.

2. At social services
Ask to see a social worker, if possible one with responsibility for your age group.

Don't be put off by the first person that you meet – remember that you have a right to a proper interview.

Ask for a child in need assessment under Section 20(3) of the Children Act

At first you might not get an interview. Lots of social workers don't know about this part of the Act, but you do – so don't give up.

3. Your child in need interview
Explain to the social worker as much as possible about your situation or as much as you feel able.

Throughout your interview –
Remember that you have a right to be heard.
Remember that what you say should be believed.
Remember that you can be helped without your parents agreeing – social services don't have to contact your parents if you don't want them to. Sorting things out with your family so you can go back isn't their only duty to you – if you can't return home or don't want to contact your family, be clear about this and don't be pressurised into doing something you don't want to.

4. Ask for a copy of your assessment in writing. Why?
It might help you make sure that you get the right service. Some social services might try and say you're not a child in need because they don't have much money – if you ask them to write down why they think you're not in need, then you can challenge them properly.

5. So you're a child in need. What now?
Getting somewhere to live
Make sure you tell them clearly what you want – a hostel place for a while or your own flat.

What if I'm offered a children's home or nothing?

- If this is okay for a while, then fine.
- If not, then tell social services it's not what you want – you want more independence.
- Social services have a duty to draw up a plan explaining how you are going to be prepared for independence Get an advice worker to help you tell them what you want included.

Want your own council flat?

- You may have a right to this from the housing department – get an advice worker to help you ask for this.
- Social services can also ask the housing department for your own place under the Children Act (section 27) – ask them to sort this out for you.
- Get an advice worker to help you go through what you need – supported hostels, bed and breakfast, supported landladies etc.

6. What about support?

What does support mean?

It can mean a bit of help sorting your bills out, helping you budget your money, or helping you deal with any problems you might have.

What sort of support do you want?

Get an advice worker to help you decide what is best for you.

7. But I don't want a social worker so what's the point?

Fine – social services can ask a range of people to help you apart from social workers.

If in doubt, ask an advice worker to help you sort out the best people for you.

What if I'm not listened to?

What if I don't get any help from social services?

Get an advice worker to help you make a complaint.

Is it all worth it? Yes, in the end you should get the help you need.

Remember. If in doubt – get help. It will make it much easier. Don't give up.

The law about leaving home

Under 16

By law, a young person under the age of 16 cannot live on an independent basis.

16 and 17 year-olds

Young people need their parents' or guardians' permission to leave home (except in Scotland). The police need to ensure they are in a place of safety.

Young people in care

They are not allowed to leave until the local authority releases them, normally when they are aged 16–18.

18 and over

Legally they are able to leave home, get married, vote . . . etc.

If you are under 16

Legally, you are still a child and your parent, guardian or local authority is responsible for you. If you leave home or care you will be sent back, unless it may be dangerous for you.

The law is very strict about not allowing you to work full time and you will find it impossible to claim any benefits or rent somewhere to live.

The best advice – talk to someone. If you cannot talk to your parents, carer or social worker, try talking to other relatives, a teacher, a close friend or one of your friends' parents.

There are some very good reasons for running away. If you are in trouble or forced to leave home suddenly, your local authority social services department will help you. The police may also help you. Hanging around on the streets, especially if you are alone, can be very dangerous and frightening.

Young, homeless, broke?

This is how you claim. It may seem a waste of time but you could get money at the end of it

Help with rent

Housing benefit

Everyone who is paying rent can claim Housing Benefit. You don't have to be on Income Support. You should claim this through the council Housing Benefit department.

These departments are well known for taking ages to sort a claim out. If you wait more than 14 days, claim a 'payment on account'. They may try to fob you off – don't let them, you are entitled to this money.

Rent-in-advance

You can claim this through the Social Fund if you are on Income Support. But, you will not be top of the list – don't bet on getting this. But have a go.

A step-by-step guide to claiming

Step 1 – Go to your nearest careers office to register for YT.

Step 2 – Then to the nearest Unemployment Benefit Office to get a form B1.

Step 3 – Take the B1 to the DSS office that covers your address or where you slept the night before.

- If possible fill in the form with someone who knows what they are doing and take a friend or adviser with you to the DSS.

Step 4 – Once you are at the DSS they will arrange an interview. Insist on an immediate interview.

- If they won't give you one then ask about a Crisis Loan.

Step 5 – The interview – there should be a special person to interview you – ask to see them.

You will be asked lots of questions about why you are not at home, why you left, can you go back?

Be prepared and don't be put off. Remember to keep your cool and

don't be pressurised into going home, if it's not right for you.

Take a friend or adviser. Be ready for a long wait, take identification and your national insurance number, if possible (you can still claim without it). Ask for a private room.

Keep in mind the sort of questions you will be asked and don't let them fob you off.

If you are homeless

You are entitled to benefit the same as anyone else but the system is made harder for you.

There is other help. If you need housing or support go to your local social services department. They have a duty to help you (especially if you are homeless or about to become homeless). This is under the new Children Act.

There's also the Social Fund

There's three parts to it.

- Crisis Loans – You don't have to be on benefit to claim this. If you are totally broke this may give you some money to tide you over. But you will have to repay it.
- Budgeting Loan – You have to be on Income Support. They are repayable and again young people are a low priority.
- Grants – Again you have to be on Income Support and if you can make a good case you may be lucky.

Setting up home after leaving care is seen as a priority claim.

Make a claim anyway. You have a right to this benefit.

- If you have just left school and live away from home you can get money for up to 4 months (depending on when you leave). This will stop as soon as a YT place comes up.
- You may automatically qualify for benefit – if you are a single parent, a carer, if you have a disability, or are a refugee learning English.
- If you can show that you will suffer without benefit you could get severe hardship money.

What's that?

It's basic income support. The DSS will ask – Can anyone else help you? Are you homeless or threatened with it? Are you ill or have a disability? Are you pregnant?

If they decide YES then you will be paid for a short period (2–6 weeks). But then you have to go back for more. Is it worth it? Yes – it's money.

Get help, get advice

Where from?

Every major city and town has agencies and centres that can give you good advice and help you get money and somewhere to live.

Use them – they have been set up for you!

- If you don't know where to look try the CAB – they may be able to help or put you in touch with someone who can.

The message is to be prepared and do not do it alone.

For more leaflets contact:
CHAR
5 –15 Cromer Street
London WC1H 8LS
Tel: 0171-833 2071

Stigma turns screw on unemployed

James Meikle meets men without homes who are no longer without hope

Malcolm had his head 'kicked in' while sleeping rough under cardboard in a multi-storey car park in Worthing, Sussex, over the winter.

He had spent two years wandering along the South Coast, nine months of it without even hostel accommodation, after a broken relationship quickly followed a broken 30-year marriage. His business as a contractor laying pipes and manholes for British Telecom had folded, and he had lost his home.

'I was always trying to find a job, but every time you apply, if you are in a hostel or have no fixed address no one wants to know you. You get such a stigma attached to you when you are homeless.'

After the attack and a night in hospital, Malcolm, aged 54, unable to find a room locally, walked on in search of a roof and found one in Crawley. The open house there has single and double rooms catering for 18 homeless people in converted building site cabins, relics of the Channel Tunnel construction. A separate block houses lavatories, showers and laundry. Meals and social areas are in the Crawley Resources Centre next door.

'I have been here eight weeks and things are working very well. I have been in hostels where if you come back with even the smell of a drink, you are out on the street for 24 hours. It is like prison.

More than 100 people have stayed at the open house in a year

'Here we have our own bedroom. If we go out we leave the key in the office and if we want to go for a drink with people outside, no one stigmatises you.'

A housing association has just interviewed Malcolm to consider offering more permanent accommodation. 'Once I get a place of my own, I can start finding work again. There are thousands of people out there who have fallen on hard times.'

David, a 50-year-old alcoholic, unemployed for five years, has been in and out of hostels since leaving the 'living hell' created by noisy and threatening neighbours in Bognor a year ago.

After three months at Crawley, he says: 'It is the first place I can see something happening. I am getting hospital treatment for an industrial injury I suffered to my back when I was working on a dustcart in Eastbourne. On the street you have got to keep walking, and I can only walk about 100 yards before the pain is so bad I have to stop.

'I am attending Alcoholics Anonymous meetings. I have had my lapses but I am quite pleased with the way things are going.' The local housing association has just interviewed him.

More than 100 people have stayed at the open house in a year, half of them local. It helps people sleeping rough at Gatwick airport nearby and has been used by asylum seekers.

Working practice

James Meikle on jobs for homeless

The vacancy signs in the window are like any other high street recruitment agency's; for sales assistants, audio-secretaries, filing clerks, partly qualified accountants or chefs. But these are jobs on offer to homeless people – the type of applicants many agencies and employers might not even look at, because there is no permanent address on the curriculum vitae. Streets Ahead, the first jobs agency for homeless people, prepares to fire the latest shot in the battle to prove to commercial companies that the out-of-luck and out-of-a-home can help the business bottom-line, not just be recipients of tea-and-sympathy charity.

Its office opposite the tube station in Holborn, central London, opened last month. Although so far none of the callers has found a permanent job, it is building up a 'bank' of suitably-qualified applicants and employers.

Within four years, it aims to have found 7,500 people full-time or part-time employment. Its backers hope by then to have at least helped spawn similar projects elsewhere, so that traditional agencies will feel sufficiently worried by the competition to re-think attitudes.

Building up job-seeking skills and suitable qualifications is just part of the challenge. There is talk of setting up a 'clothes library' where applicants can borrow the necessary gear, ranging from a suit to help them look smart in the office to the uniform and hats that are needed in the catering industry.

Some jobseekers – and they can walk in off the street provided they fulfil the need criteria – may need help with transport costs for interviews, while others may require assistance with rent, even in hostels or longer-term accommodation.

Centrepoint, the youth homeless agency running the project, with the Peabody Trust, already has a 'charitable rebate' enabling it to cushion the steep reductions in housing benefit that accompany the move off the dole queue into work. But other agencies referring applicants may find such assistance beyond them.

Within four years, it aims to have found 7,500 people full-time or part-time employment

Shane Hickey, the manager of Streets Ahead, used to work for the Alfred Marks chain. 'There will be key areas, financial, accountancy, secretarial, care, nursing, retail and catering,' he says. 'I am not here just to get people into low-paid jobs. This is going to be the biggest, most revolutionary thing happening in the recruitment market. We have had 55–60 people through the door. They have given their commitment and though it may be they still need their recruitment counselling and training, they have taken their first step.

'Even if homeless people get over the door in traditional agencies, they come up against six or seven others whose CVs don't have the term "homeless"'

'Employers have a social conscience and want to be seen to be helping. But they can save money too. Provided we get the right level of applicants and provide the right level of service, this can develop money that can go back into services for the homeless.'

This is important. Organisers of the scheme, which grew out of co-operation between the Homeless Network of charities and voluntary groups, the local training and enterprise council CenTEC, recruitment agency Blue Arrow, and Westminster council, were acutely conscious that they might be accused of 'creaming off' the most 'recruitable' homeless, leaving others without the time, effort and training they needed to find a way into the jobs market.

To begin with, the subsidies will help pay training costs and keep recruitment fees to employers substantially lower than the 14 to 22 per cent of annual salary charged by other agencies. But the target is to make it first self-financing, and then run up surpluses that can be spent elsewhere.

Ian Brady, deputy chief executive of Centrepoint, said: 'Even if homeless people get over the door in traditional agencies, they come up against six or seven others whose CVs don't have the term "homeless" on it. Not everyone here will get a job but if someone is referred to use who is not "job ready", we can offer vocational guidance, training and try to find work experience.

'Employers want to offer their jobs, but we don't want to build up expectations until we have built up the skill base. This is a long-haul project. It is not going to work in the first couple of weeks of operation.'

Runaways

A study by ChildLine

Introduction

Every year, thousands of children and young people run away. It is difficult to establish precise numbers, but one study has suggested that there were 102,000 missing person incidents involving 43,000 children under 18 in Scotland and England in 1990 (Abrahams and Mungall, 1992). Other research (Newmann, 1989) estimated that every year as many as 98,000 missing person incidents involving children under the age of 18 occur in the UK.

Contrary to popular belief, previous research shows that young people do not run away in search of the bright lights of London; they are more likely to be running from troubles and problems at home, wanting to escape what has become an intolerable situation. Many return soon, a few remain away for long periods of time.

Those who stay away for weeks or months face enormous difficulties. Since 1988, 16 and 17 year-olds have not been entitled to income support, and young people between 18 and 24 are only entitled to a lower rate. In addition, recent government decisions have cut housing benefit to young people. With no means of claiming benefit and little likelihood of being able to earn money, young runaways and homeless are often destitute; some use other means of earning money, like casual work, prostitution, drugs dealing or begging. Often the only time information comes to light about young runaways is when they come to the attention of the police or statutory agencies.

Some young people find refuge in the safe houses and street projects run by voluntary organisations, who give help, support and advice to young runaways and young homeless; however there are still far too few projects scattered around the country to reach more than a fraction of the many young people who run away and are unable or unwilling to turn to the statutory sector for help. There are no safe houses for under-age children in Scotland; there is one each in London, Leeds, Dorset and Wales. In order to get into other homeless projects, young people have to hide their age.

Between March 1994 and April 1995 ChildLine counselled 2,205 children who had either run away or been thrown out or evicted by their parents or guardians. This is approximately 180 children every month. This section of the report is based on an analysis of these calls, together with a more detailed look at a month's sample of 206 calls.

Who runs away?

The term 'runaways' is traditionally used – and is used here – to describe three categories of children and young people: those who leave their parental homes or care placements without permission, those who are thrown out of their homes by their parents or carers, and those who are aged between 16 and 18 with nowhere to live.

Children under 16 are legally required to be in the care and control of their parents or legal guardian. These children are not legally able to leave this care whether they have run away or have been thrown out by their parents or carers.

The majority of children (1,381) contacting ChildLine had run away from their parental homes. But a significant minority (107) had run away from either foster care or a residential home. Research has shown that although the majority of children run away from their parental homes, a higher-than-average proportion of children run away from care. So, although approximately 1 per cent of all children in England are in care, 7 per cent of the children contacting ChildLine about running away had run from their care placements.

The majority of children contacting ChildLine because they had run away were adolescents. Three-quarters of children who gave their age were between 13 and 16 years old. Running away is overwhelmingly a problem of middle to late adolescence. This may be for a number of reasons: younger children may find the idea of leaving their homes very frightening, having less experience of independence than adolescents, and they may not have the peer support systems that older children have developed which may provide them with somewhere temporary to stay. Nevertheless a number of younger children did contact ChildLine after running away; 307 children between the ages of nine and 12, and 18 between five and eight years old.

The majority (64%) of callers were girls, a ratio of 1.8 girls to one boy. The overall ratio of girls to boys contacting ChildLine is four to one. The higher-than-average percentage of boys contacting ChildLine about running away may imply that it is easier for boys to seek help once their problems have reached a crisis point such as having no safe place to stay.

The figures from our month's samples tell a similar story. In one month, 206 children contacted ChildLine because they had nowhere to stay: 138 had run away and 68 had been thrown out. Sixty-seven per cent of children were aged between 13 and 16, with 68 per cent being girls.

Why children run away

Children told ChildLine again and again that they ran away from their parental homes because of problems in their relationship with members of their family, or because of abuse. Thirty-six per cent (793) of runaway and homeless children told counsellors that there were difficulties with their family relationships, and 34 per cent (762) that they had been abused. Of those 762 children, 593 children talked of physical abuse, 143 reported sexual abuse and 26 children said they had run away because they were experiencing both sexual and physical abuse.

Other reasons for running away included being pregnant, experiencing problems at school, bullying and experiencing domestic violence. Frequently children gave more than one reason for running away.

Children who ran away from care told counsellors of arguments, unfair restrictions, time curfews, physical abuse and, sometimes, a wish to return home to one or both of their birth parents. Some of these children had already experienced multiple care placements – one girl had been in 11 foster homes; she said, 'I'm so unhappy I could kill myself.' She eventually agreed to phone her foster parents.

In the month's sample, the reasons given to counsellors for running away were very similar to those found within the year's statistics; 78 (38%) children reported family relationship problems, 54 (26%) physical abuse, 15 (7%) sexual abuse and a further two children reported both. In addition 17 children (8%) had run away because of problems with being in care.

• The above is an extract from *Children at crisis point – A study by ChildLine*. See page 39 for address details.

Analysis of missing persons cases

- An estimated 250,000 people go missing in the UK every year.
- Missing people come from all age groups, racial backgrounds, differing social and income groups, and from all areas.
- Age analyses of cases handled, indicate that the highest proportion of females who go missing are under the age of 17 but all age groups are affected.
- The highest proportion of males who go missing are between the ages of 36 to 50 years old but all age groups are affected.
- Many are young people seeking to leave parents, schooling and other real or perceived sources of pressure.
- A high proportion of missing person cases are aged over 65. Reports show that they have been suffering from the effects associated with old age, in particular Alzheimer's, Senile Dementia and loss of memory.
- There are a wide variety of reasons why people go missing, including: problems at home, problems at work, long-term stress, unhappiness, debts, redundancy, illness, injury, alcohol, glue-sniffing, drugs, abduction, school, foul play, abuse, bullying, unexpected impulse and choice.
- Only 5% of the cases National Missing Persons Helpline (NMPH) deal with are found dead, whether from accident, suicide, natural causes or foul-play.

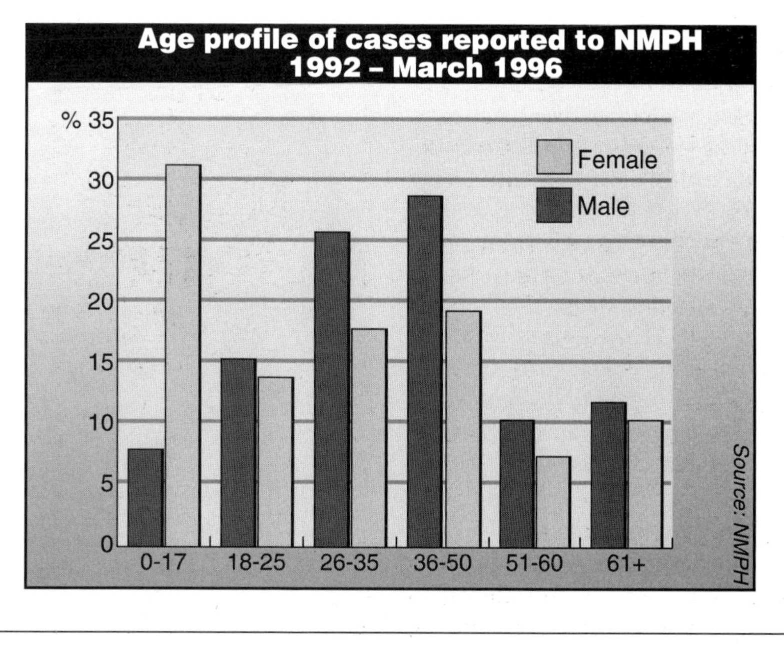

Young people's reasons for running away

An extract from *Runaways – Exploding the myths*

Certain factors relevant to the motivations of runaways repeatedly came to notice during the course of the study and through wider experience, and these are reported and discussed here. This is not complete picture because every young person acts for their own reasons and these can best be established by interviewing the young person after the running away. In some cases the reason for running away was not entered on the missing persons form.

Runaways from home

Arguments are often the trigger

Rows within the family frequently appear to be the immediate precursors of decisions to run away. In the study the subjects of these arguments included staying out late and whether young people were or were not to be allowed to attend parties, pop concerts etc.; arguments with siblings; young people's offending behaviour; abuse of alcohol or drugs; and truancy from school and other school-related problems, including exclusions (both temporary and permanent), conflict with teachers and other pupils, alleged thefts and exam failures.

Running away after being 'grounded'

Some young people ran away apparently in protest after having been punished by parents for some misdemeanour, quite often speaking out after having supposedly been 'grounded'. There seemed to be an element of bravado in many of these escapades, especially when they involved two or more friends camping out for the night.

Gender differences

Gender differences were sometimes apparent in the subjects about which arguments with parents took place; rows about partners and staying out late predominantly seemed to involve young women. Conversely, concerns about young men being out of control – out late at night or out of school – seemed often to focus on fears that they might become involved in crime. It is perhaps surprising that these gender stereotypes should still retain their power in the 1990s.

Deeper-seated conflicts between parents and children

In many cases it seems that whilst an argument triggered the decision to run away, underlying tensions about young people's chosen lifestyles were responsible at a deeper level for conflicts with parents. This is hardly surprising since according to the study findings most runaways are in their mid-teens, precisely the ages at which young people are struggling to create their own identities separate from those of their parents.

In a noticeable proportion of cases in the study young people appeared simply to be drifting away from their families, possibly spending more nights of the week sleeping at friends' houses than at home.

In these situations no specific incident generally appeared to have triggered the decision of parents or other carers to report the young person missing to the police, apart from the feeling that she or he had 'gone too far' and that some control over their behaviour needed to be reasserted.

It is difficult to see how simply returning the young person home would be likely to improve matters in these situations. Many of these young people were 16 or 17 and therefore near the age of being able to leave home legally with or without parental consent (or beyond it in the cases of those from Scotland). A smaller number were only 13 or 14, and it might be that they and their families would need some outside help if they were to negotiate a mutually acceptable way of living together.

Running away to avoid difficult encounters

Some young people included in the study appeared to run away in order

to avoid difficult encounters with parents about their behaviour 'outside' home. This was apparent in the cases of some young people in the study who had come to the notice of police and had been charged with committing offences, and of others who were involved in what they considered to be serious trouble at school and knew that the school had contacted home.

A noticeable proportion of runaways in the study also seemed to have run away in a direct attempt to avoid court cases and police cautions.

Running away and theft from home
In a small number of cases in the study young people had left having taken large amounts of money from home. It was usually unclear whether the theft and fear of its discovery was the motive for the young person deciding to run away, or whether the money was taken to subsidise being away from home.

Differences in the ways that decisions to leave are made
In some cases included in the study the decision to leave seemed to have been taken calmly and could be viewed as a very mature response to a difficult situation at home or in young people's personal lives. Some left having written notes to the effect that they needed some space to sort themselves out and would return after a few days. Conversely, a few left notes threatening suicide or that they would never return; these youngsters were invariably home again within a short period of time.

Runaways in serious crisis
A small but significant proportion of young people reported to have run away from home in the study were quite clearly in a state of personal crisis and some were a serious risk to themselves. One young person reported missing during the September 1990 study was found to have committed suicide.

A very few runaways included in the study appeared to be following a fixed pattern of repeatedly running to places where they appeared deliberately to put themselves at risk. These runaways were well known to the statutory social services and to the police.

16 and 17 year-old runaways and unemployment
An additional perspective on the individual motivations of young people who run away from home is provided by the observation that the overwhelming majority of reported runaways aged 16 and 17 from home and care in the study were unemployed.

The absence of secure full-time employment would be unlikely in itself to motivate a young person to run away, but being happily employed or engaged in higher education may be factors which help to 'anchor' a young person, and make it less likely that she or he will decide to run away, if only for practical reasons.

The experience of abuse as a reason for running away
This study generated only a few examples of abuse at home clearly motivating a young person to run away. However, this issue would only have come to notice in the study if one of two situations had occurred and was noted on the relevant cancellation form: firstly, if a returned runaway disclosed that she or he had been abused at home, if and when interviewed by police; and secondly, if some other evidence of abuse came to police attention during investigation of the missing person case.

The experience of many of those who work directly with runaways is that abuse at home (and in care) is quite often said by young people to be one of their reasons for having run away. It would therefore be quite inappropriate to assume on the basis of this study that abuse at home is only rarely a reason for young people running away.

• The above is an extract from *Runaways – Exploding the myths* published by NCH Action for Children. See page 39 for address details.

Running away experiences

An extract from *Nowhere to Hide*

Where the young people ran from

The majority of the young people had run away from within greater London, with just over a quarter running from outside their local area. Those who had come to London had run from a variety of locations throughout England. However, the majority had run away from the south-west or south-east, with 13 per cent running from the midlands or northern England.

Extent of running away

The majority, 71 per cent of the 161 who responded, had run away before, only 29 per cent (46) had run away for the first time.

Reason for past running

The majority (60 of the 88 who responded) of young people who had run away before stated that the reasons they had run in the past were the same reasons they had run away this time. Twenty-eight had run away in the past because of different problems.

Frequency of past running

A significant number (27) of the young people had run away repeatedly, often for the same reasons they had run in the past. This indicates that for some, problems did not decrease as a result of their running away. Twenty-one young people had only run away once before and 16 had run away twice.

Length of time away

The majority of young people who had run to London from outside their local area were referred to the Refuge before having to spend the night in London. However, a significant minority had been in London for over three weeks. Nearly half of those who had run to London from outside their local area had only been in London for one day before being referred to the Refuge. Almost a third had been in London for between two and seven days, and only a minority for over a week before referral. However, this should be viewed in the context of the substantial risks young people face once they have run away.

Extent of running away alone or with others

Most of the young people had run away on their own, only a minority had run away with somebody else, usually a friend, despite the commonly held belief that young people run away in groups. Three-quarters (74 per cent) arrived at the Refuge alone. Only a third of young people arrived with other runaways. The majority, 32 young people who arrived accompanied at the Refuge, were with only one other person, eight came with two and seven with three others.

Places the young people stayed while away

Young people were asked where else they had stayed since they had been away. Almost half had experienced dangerous circumstances before they arrived at the Refuge. Twenty-four per cent had slept rough and 7 per cent had stayed in a squat. A fifth had stayed with friends they knew before running away, and 8 per cent had stayed with people they had met since running away. They had also approached services intended for homeless people, with 11 per cent staying in a hostel and 6 per cent

Running away

Number of times the young person had run away

	%
Once	27
Twice	16
3–7 times	23
8–14 times	15
15–21 times	8
22 –28 times	3
29–56 times	8
More than 57 times	1
Total	100

Number of days spent in London before being referred to the Refuge if from outside the area

	%
No days	4
1 day	49
2–7 days	33
8–14 days	4
15–21 days	4
22 days or more	6
Total	100

All places stayed while away

	%
Slept rough	24
Friends known before running away	21
Hostel	11
Shelter	6
Persons not known before running	8
Parents	8
Squat	7
Other relatives	3

People approached for advice and assistance

	%
Friends	10
Social workers	9
Relatives apart from parents	2
Institutional staff	2
Youth worker	1
Police	1
Teacher	1
Other	10

staying in a shelter. Five young people had also stayed at the homes of family members with whom they did not usually live.

Seeking advice before running

The majority (62 per cent) of the young people had not approached anyone for advice about their problems before running away (159 responded). Nineteen young people approached their peers for advice and 18 approached a social worker. This may reflect the fact that running is rarely a planned event.

Young persons' evaluation of responses from social services and peer group

Although the number of young people in each of these categories is small they do provide some insight into the responses they received upon seeking advice. Nine of the young people who approached a social worker for advice felt that the social worker was either unwilling to listen or did not believe them. Only five said they received advice and one was offered practical help by the social worker. Thirteen who approached their friends stated they were either offered advice or practical help and only one young person said they received a negative response.

• The above is an extract from *Nowhere to Hide*, published by Centrepoint. See page 39 for address details.

Nowhere to hide

Information from Centrepoint

Reasons the young people ran away

Conflict and arguments were identified as the main reason for running by almost half of the young people but a significant minority were also running from abuse, particularly physical abuse. Physical abuse was cited by 10 per cent as a main reason for running made up of 20 young people, 18 of whom were running from the parental home. Overall, 17 per cent of young people cited abuse as the main reason they had taken flight. Only a minority had been told to leave the place they were living by their parents or carers. These were the main reasons why young people were running from their parental home whereas bullying and disliking the place they were living in accounted for those running from the care system.

All reasons for running away

The young people were also asked to identify all the reasons they had run away. When we compare all reasons with main reasons, within almost every category there is an absolute increase in the number of young people experiencing that problem, indicating the existence of multiple problems.

Two-thirds identified the presence of conflict and arguments in their lives as a contributing factor in their decision to run away. The impact of abuse on their lives becomes apparent when all reasons for running are considered. Two-fifths (39 young people) reported physical abuse with 11 experiencing emotional abuse and 11 experiencing sexual abuse. Thirty-two young people stated they disliked the place they were living in, and 19 cited bullying as a factor in their decision to run away. The response rates are low but the figures may under-estimate the extent of abuse. Research has shown that young people are not always willing to divulge this information without the time to develop a sense of trust in staff (Strathdee 1992).

• The above is an extract from *Nowhere to Hide – Giving young runaways a voice*, published by Centrepoint. See page 39 for address details.

Main reason the young person ran

	%
Conflict and arguments	49
Physical abuse	13
Disliked place	10
Told to leave/ evicted	5
Bullying	4
Sexual abuse	3
In trouble	3
Emotional abuse	1
Return to own area	1
Racial harassment/ violence	1
Other	10
Total	100

All reasons for running away

	%
Conflict and arguments	43
Physical violence	20
Disliked place	16
Bullying	10
In trouble	7
Emotional abuse	6
Sexual abuse	6
Told to leave/ evicted	3
Racial harassment/ violence	3
Return to own area	1
Return home	1
*Total	116

* Totals do not add up to 100 per cent as more than one answer could be given

The National Missing Persons Helpline – Factfile 1996

The National Missing Persons Helpline (NMPH) was established in 1992 to advise and support the families of those who go missing. It gives priority to the vulnerable – the very young, the old, the sick and distressed. It is a charity entirely dependent on voluntary donations.

The scale of the problem

More than 250,000 people are reported missing in the UK each year. More than 100,000 (40%) are under 18. The vast majority return safe and sound within 72 hours – but thousands do not. The NMPH has over 14,000 files open and more are added every day. It receives more than 80,000 calls per year. Two out of every three cases publicised by the Helpline are resolved.[1]

Who goes missing

Opinions differ on who counts as a missing person. The police do not look for people except in cases of vulnerability or crime. The Salvation Army's Family Tracing Service concentrates on blood relatives and brings thousands back together each year, but does not handle other categories.[2]

Other specialised agencies, official and voluntary, deal with various aspects of the missing persons phenomenon, but none has an overview of the problem as a whole. There is no central or single source of general or statistical information on a growing social problem which causes much distress to the absent and those they leave behind alike.

Young people

More is known about those under 18 who go missing than any other group. Some 43,000 of these generate about 100,000 missing person reports per year. One-third of young runaways account for three-quarters of these incidents. Seven per cent of young absentees are under 12; the majority are 14–16.[3]

Nearly two-thirds of young absentees run away from residential care; less than a quarter run from home. Less than 1% of the young population is in residential care, but 30% of young runaways come from there.

Of those under 18 who go missing, 55% are boys, according to one survey.[3] But twice as many girls are reported missing to the Helpline as boys.

One disturbing indication of what happens to young people who absent themselves is the fact that nearly 1,500 people under 18 were convicted, and 1,800 cautioned, for prostitution and related offences in the five years from 1989 to 1993. In recent local surveys of young runaways, 20% in Manchester and 15% in Birmingham reported involvement in prostitution.[4]

Nearly 1,000 children per year are abducted from the UK, mostly by a parent from a broken marriage.[5]

Adult 'mispers'

Very little general information exists on missing adults. The NMPH has

begun researching this area because (a) there is a dearth of statistical information and analysis on missing persons and (b) the Helpline itself possesses more general information on its unique database than any other organisation. But, although its thousands of files constitute an unusually large sample, it is a random, self-selecting one, determined almost wholly by those who decide to report someone missing to the NMPH.

With this proviso, the Helpline's database indicated that:

- the younger the missing adult, the more likely (s)he is to turn up;
- males aged 23 to 32 are more likely to disappear than any other group (the peak ages are 28 and 29);
- female adults are more likely to go missing the younger they are (the peak ages are 26 and 27);
- more people go missing from London (29%) and the South East (24%) than any other UK region;
- more people go missing in October than in any other month (13%) and more turn up in March than any other month (14.5%)
- people born on a Tuesday are most likely to go missing!

Why they go missing

Reasons for going missing vary widely. A large body of empirical information gives some clear pointers. Problems at home, work or school which can drive people to leave include:

- abuse (physical and/or sexual)
- debt
- domestic dispute
- illness
- general anxiety or stress
- depression or other mental illness
- amnesia, senility or Alzheimer's disease
- alcohol, drug or solvent misuse
- abduction (most feared but least likely) or
- just because they feel like it.

It should not be forgotten that people over 18 are at liberty to choose to go away and break off contact. The NMPH therefore guarantees confidentiality to seekers and found alike; its commitment to confidentiality has won the respect of police around the country. It recognises the right to stay out of touch and can forward an 'alive and well' message to put relatives' minds at rest without revealing the sender's whereabouts.

How the NMPH works

The charity operates a nationwide Freecall telephone service 24 hours a day, seven days a week, on 0500 700 700. It also operates the confidential 'Message Home' service on Freecall 0500 700 740. The NMPH charges no fee because many families of missing people cannot afford one. But donations are encouraged because the Helpline needs £750,000 a year just to keep ticking over.

Details of all those recorded as missing by the NMPH go into its computerised database. Callers reporting non-urgent cases may be referred to other organisations or else advised on how to look for someone themselves.

The Helpline supports the distressed and tries to reunite families by searching for vulnerable missing people via its network of contacts and sources, official and unofficial, throughout the UK and beyond. It also operates a special, technologically advanced 'ageing' computer to help trace the long-term missing, especially children, from dated photographs.

The Helpline used its database to assist the police in identifying four of the victims of Frederick and Rosemary West in the Gloucester serial-murder case. In the process it was also able to reunite some 120 families who feared that a young female relative had been murdered.

Helpline people

The National Missing Persons Helpline has more than fifty unpaid volunteers and a staff of 21 salaried employees from the most varied backgrounds. They are led by two sisters, Mrs Janet Newman and Mrs Mary Asprey, who were both honoured with the OBE in 1995 – only three years after they co-founded the charity in a room in Janet's house. Today it operates from a donated office of 2,000 square feet in south-west London.

The price of success

The main threat to the Helpline's future is that it has become a victim of its own success. As its reputation grows and spreads, more and more people turn to it for help in seeking lost ones, which means ever-growing expense.

Its founders have been honoured by the Queen and praised in Parliament by the Prime Minister, but the Helpline has received hardly any compensation for its increasingly important social contribution.

The NMPH seeks £1.5 million to stabilise its finances. It relies heavily on unpaid volunteers, but needs to expand its salaried staff in order to meet the relentlessly rising demand for its free service to missing people and their families.

- The National Missing Persons Helpline tel: 0181 392 2000. 'Message Home' tel: 0500 700 740.

References:
1 NMPH
2 Salvation Army 1992–3
3 National Children's Home/Metropolitan Police/Police Foundation joint study 1992
4 Children's Society Report 1994
5 NMPH

Freecall Message Home

A confidential FREECALL helpline for those who have run away to send a message home and/or get confidential help and advice.

What is *FREE*CALL MESSAGE HOME?

Anyone who has left home or run away can telephone the *FREECALL* **MESSAGE HOME** helpline and leave a message to be passed on to a relative, social worker or friend.

Often young people who have left home or run away feel they cannot make direct contact with their home, even to phone someone to tell them they are alive and safe. This is where the **MESSAGE HOME** helpline can send a message to their relative, social worker or friend on their behalf and try to open 'a line of communication'.

This is often the first step to positive communication between all parties.

Callers can also ask for confidential help and advice, particularly young people who have run away from home.

What makes the service so special?

The helpline is a FREECALL service which means callers do not need any money to telephone.

It is a national helpline and can pass on messages and help callers anywhere in the United Kingdom.

Confidentially – callers do not have to give any personal details if they do not want and there is no threat of tracing a call.

A message can be left with the helpline seven days a week, 24 hours a day.

Message Home is used . . .

By those who have run away from care:

'Sorry we have run away . . . as soon as we get some money we want to come back, but we are scared.'

By those escaping family problems:
'I am still alive, but want no contact with my dad as I am better off without him.'

By those unsure how their parents will react:
'Please ask them if I can come back home . . . I miss them.'

*FREE*CALL MESSAGE HOME

- It is estimated that around 43,000 people under 17 run away every year in England and Scotland alone.
- 68% of runaways are aged 14–16, 7% are 11 or younger.
- 45% of runaways are girls.

There is no other telephone helpline service, either regionally or nationally, which provides a confidential 24-hour National *FREECALL* **MESSAGE HOME** and support service for people who have left home, particularly young runaways who want help, advice and/or to send a message home . . .

• *FREECALL* **MESSAGE HOME** 0500 700 740. Office telephone 0181 876 7763.

Runaways

Exploding the myths

What is a runaway?

For the purposes of the project a runaway was defined as: a young person aged under 18 who has left home or local authority care without agreement and has stayed away for a 'significant period of time', the length of time regarded as significant being related to the age of the runaway. For example it might be much more significant if a 5 year-old stayed away of her or his own accord for 3 hours than if a 16 year-old did so.

A 'runaway' is not the same as a 'young homeless person'. Some runaways become homeless, and some young homeless people have run away, but the terms are not synonymous: 'runaway' relates to a mode of departure, 'homeless' to a state of being (without a home).

The essence of the term 'runaway' is that she or he is away without consent, explicit or otherwise. A young person aged under 16 cannot live legally on an independent basis in Great Britain. Therefore the concept of a 14 year-old homeless youth is a legal nonsense; she or he is either a runaway who happens to be homeless, or a 'throwaway – someone who has been thrown out by her or his parents or carers.

In England and Wales the ages of 16 and 17 are a 'grey area', since although parents theoretically have the right to refuse to allow a son or daughter to leave home, this right is difficult to enforce. A 16 or 17 year-old in England and Wales may therefore be a runaway or a throwaway, or homeless, or both. In Scotland a 16 year-old may legally leave home with or without parental consent.

Summary of key findings

- Runaways should not be confused with the young single homeless. There is a difference which depends on age, and whether or not the young person is allowed to live independently.
- An estimated 43,000 young people, generating over 100,000 incidents, ran away in England and Scotland in 1990.
- Overall, the majority of runaways were in the 14–16 age group. Over 7% of individual runaways, of whom most were boys running from home, were aged 11 or less.
- 65% of individual runaways ran away only once during the year: 35% ran more than once, accounting for 73% of runaway incidents.
- Individuals from residential care were more likely to run away repeatedly than those from home: 62% compared to 23%. 20% of those who ran repeatedly from care compared to 2% from home were absent 10 times.
- 62% of runaway incidents of known duration lasted up to 24 hours; 77% for up to 48 hours. Only 2% lasted for more than 14 days.
- The number of runaways from residential establishments was disproportionate to the percentage of the population in residential care: 30% compared to less than 1%.
- 96% of care runaways were from residential establishments.
- Only a small percentage of care runaways were from foster placements. They were vastly under-represented in comparison to the proportion of the total care population in foster care: 4% compared to over 60%.
- Some types of care establishment produced larger numbers of runaway incidents than others. 58% of runaway incidents from residential care were from 40 establishments.
- Less than 1% of runaway incidents resulted in the young person going to London. In only 2% of cases did young people leave their home area.
- Running away occurred in all areas, rural and urban, but much higher numbers ran from disadvantaged areas.
- A disproportionately large number of runaways in the London study had already been identified as vulnerable.
- Overall, 55% of individuals were boys and 45% girls.
- 69% of runaway incidents in the London survey resulted in young people returning of their own accord.
- In most areas records of how often young people ran away were not kept by relevant agencies or were not easily accessible.
- In most areas there was an apparent lack of co-ordination between social work agencies and the police in relation to the issue of running away.
- Little had been done in most areas to find out why so many young people run from care and to seek solutions.
- It is apparent that the planned national register of missing persons will not deal adequately with the issue of runaways.

• The above is an extract from *Runaways – Exploding the myths* published by NCH Action for Children. See page 39 for address details.

INDEX

ADDITIONAL RESOURCES

Alone in London
318 St Paul's Road
London N1 2LF
Tel: 0171 278 4224
Fax: 0171 359 9690
Works to relieve the homelessness of young people aged 16-21. To enable young people to live as indpendently as possible. Produces publications.

Centrepoint
Bewlay House
2 Swallow Place
London W1R 7AA
Tel: 0171 629 2229
Fax: 0171 409 2027
Ensures that no young person is at risk because they do not have a safe place to stay. Produces many publications on young people leaving home and homelessness. Specifically *The Leaving Home Guide*, available free from the above address.

CHAR (Housing Campaign for Single People)
1-15 Cromer Street
London WC1H 8LS
Tel: 0171 833 2071
A leading housing campaign organisation for single homeless, CHAR produces a wide range of reports, books and leaflets. Ask for their publications order form. Please note that CHAR has insufficient staff to handle student inquiries but will respond to teaher's request for information. for student enquiries.

ChildLine
2nd Floor Royal Mail Building
Studd Street
London N1 0QW
Tel: 0171 239 1000 (admin)
Fax: 0171 239 1001
ChildLine is the free, national helpline for children and young people in trouble or danger. It provides confidential phone counselling service for any child with any problem 24 hours a day. Produces publications. Children or young people can phone or write free of charge about problems of any kind. ChildLine, Freepost 1111, London N1 0BR, of telephone Freephone 0800 1111

Church Action on Poverty
Central Buildings
Oldham Street
Manchester M1 1JT
Tel: 0161 236 9321
Fax: 0161 237 5359
An ecumenical organisation whose aims are to raise awareness about the causes, extent and impact of poverty in the UK. Produce publications on poverty.

Churches' National Housing Coalition
Central Buildings
Oldham Street
Manchester M1 1JT
Tel: 0161 236 9321
Fax: 0161 237 5359
A coalition of over 500 churches, charities and housing organisations. It helps the churches to be more effective in attacking the causes of homelessness by working together. Produce factsheets, reports etc.

Crisis
1st Floor
Challenger House
42 Adler Street
London E1 1EE
Tel: 0171 377 0489
Fax: 0171 247 1525
A national charity working with single, homeless people, researching, developing and funding schemes that provide help at all stages of being homeless. Ask for their publications leaflet.

Methodist Association of Youth Clubs (MAYC)
2 Chester House
Pages Lane
Muswell Hill
London N10 1PR
Tel: 0181 444 9845
Fax: 0181 365 2471

National Housing Federation
175 Gray's Inn Road
London WC1X 8UP
Tel: 0171 278 6571
Gives aid and advice to housing associations and other charitable agencies providing housing and related services to homeless people.

National Missing Persons Helpline (NMPH)
Roebuck House
284-286 Upper Richmond Road West
London SW14 7JE
Tel: 0181 392 2000
Fax: 0181 878 7752
Works to find missing people and help them regain contact with those left behind. Provides counselling and support to families where a member has gone missing. Produces publications.

NCH Action for Children
85 Highbury Park
London N5 1UD
Tel: 0171 226 2033
Fax: 0171 226 2537
One of the UK 's leading childcare charities with 250 projects natronwide helping over 25,000 children and young peopler every year. Produces publications.

Scottish Council for Single Homeless (SCSH)
9 Forrest Road
Edinburgh EH1 2QH
Tel: 0131 226 4382
Fax: 0131 220 3107
Scotland's research and campaigning organisation on all aspects of single homelessness. Ask for their publications catalogue.

Shelter
88 Old Street
London
EC1V 9HU
Tel: 0171 253 0202
Fax: 0171 505 2169
Campaigns for decent homes that everyone can afford. Produces publications.

ACKNOWLEDGEMENTS

The publisher is grateful for permission to reproduce the following material.

While every care has been taken to trace and acknowledge copyright, the publisher tenders its apology for any accidental infringement or where copyright has proved untraceable. The publisher would be pleased to come to a suitable arrangement in any such case with the rightful owner.

Chapter One: No fixed abode

Young people and homelessness, © Shelter, October 1996, *Rites of passage*, © CHAR, *We don't choose to be homeless*, © CHAR, *Leaving home*, © Centrepoint, *1 in 20 of young are homeless*, © The Daily Mirror, September 1996, *Homelessness in England*, © Shelter, October 1996, *Young homeless people*, © Scottish Council for Single Homeless, *Hearing young people*, © National Housing Federation, October 1996, *The Crisis factsheet*, © Crisis, *Family homelessness*, © Church Action on Poverty, People Need Homes resource pack, *Homeless families 'still torn apart'*, © The Guardian, September 1996, *Homing instincts*, © The Guardian, July 1995, *Dependency with no know-how*, © The Guardian, October 1996, *Scandal – time to act*, © Methodist Children's Charity, *Sleeping rough*, © Crisis, *£4m shelters for rough sleepers*, © The Guardian, April 1996, *Are you 16 or 17 and homeless?*, © CHAR, *The law about leaving home*, © National Missing Persons Helpline, *Young, homeless, broke?*, © CHAR, *Stigma turns screw on unemployed*, © The Guardian, April 1996, *Working practice*, © The Guardian, May 1996.

Chapter Two: Runaways

Runaways, © ChildLine, *Analysis of missing persons cases*, © National Missing Persons Helpline, *Young people's reasons for running away*, © NCH Action for Children, *Running away experiences*, © Centrepoint, *Nowhere to hide*, © Centrepoint, *The National Missing Persons Helpline – Factfile 1996*, © National Missing Persons Helpline, *Freecall Message Home*, © National Missing Persons Helpline, *Runaways*, © NCH Action for Children.

Photographs and Illustrations

Pages 1, 19, 23, 30, 31: Andrew Smith / Folio Collective, pages 4, 11, 26, 34: Katherine Fleming / Folio Collective, page 6: N Martin / Folio Collective, pages 8, 22, 24: Ken Pyne.

Craig Donnellan
Cambridge
April, 1997